8-SESSION TEEN BIBLE STUDY

REVISED

MIKE & DANIEL BLACKABY

EXPERIENCING
GOD

Knowing & Doing
the Will of God

EDITORIAL TEAM

Karen Daniel
Editorial Team Leader

John Paul Basham
**Manager, Student
Ministry Publishing**

Ben Trueblood
**Director,
Student Ministry**

Kyle Wiltshire
Content Editor

Morgan Hawk
Production Editor

Kaitlin Redmond
Art Director

Published by Lifeway Press® • © 2022 Mike and Daniel Blackaby
Reprinted May 2022, Sept. 2022, Feb. 2023

ISBN 978-1-0877-2531-4 • Item 005828348

Dewey decimal classification: 227.6
Subject headings: RELIGION / Christian Ministry / Youth

To order additional copies of this resource, write to Lifeway
Resources Customer Service; 200 Powell Place, Suite 100,
Brentwood, TN 37027; fax 615-251-5933; phone toll free 800-458-
2772; order online at lifeway.com; or email orderentry@lifeway.com.

Printed in the United States of America.

Student Ministry Publishing • Lifeway Resources
200 Powell Place, Suite 100 • Brentwood, TN 37027

Table of Contents

About the Authors

MIKE BLACKABY grew up in Alberta, Canada, where he learned to snowboard and play hockey on frozen ponds. At 18 years old, Mike felt God calling him to do something that terrified him: become a pastor. He enrolled and graduated from Ambrose University before moving to North Carolina to get a master's degree from Southeastern Baptist Theological Seminary. From 2010-2018, he was a pastor for young adults near Atlanta, Georgia, while also completing his PhD in Worldview and Apologetics from the Southern Baptist Theological Seminary. He and his brother, Daniel, have co-authored two books together: *When Worlds Collide: Standing Up and Stepping Out in an Anti-God Culture* and *Seven Steps to Knowing, Doing, and Experiencing the Will of God: for Teens*. In 2018, Mike and his family moved to Vancouver Island in British Columbia to start a new church in the beautiful city of Victoria. He loves fantasy books, espresso, and playing music, as well as watching cooking shows with his wife, Sarah. Mike and Sarah have three young sons and a baby daughter.

ABOUT THE ORIGINAL AUTHORS

Experiencing God was originally published in 1990 and written by Henry Blackaby and Claude King. Henry is Mike and Daniel's grandfather. Their father, Richard Blackaby, has also made revisions over the years. *Experiencing God* has sold over seven million copies and been translated into over forty-five languages.

DANIEL BLACKABY is a storyteller and a lover of the creative arts. He is passionate about encouraging Christian artists to leverage their God-given creativity for His glory. He currently serves as the Director of Online Classes and NextGen Initiatives at Blackaby Ministries International. He speaks on cultural engagement, apologetics, and reaching the younger generations. Driven by his passion for pop culture and the arts, he launched The Collision—a multimedia ministry aimed at equipping Christians to navigate, engage, and contribute to today's culture. He has authored several books, including *When Worlds Collide: Stepping Up and Standing Out in an Anti-God Culture* and the imaginative fantasy trilogy *The Lost City Chronicles*. He holds a PhD in Christianity and the Arts and a ThM in Philosophy, Worldview, and Apologetics from the Southern Baptist Theological Seminary. He currently lives near Atlanta, Georgia, with his wife, Sarah, twin boys, Emerson and Logan, and a scruffy dog named Bilbo.

How to Use

Experiencing God provides a guided process for individuals and groups. This Bible study book includes eight weeks of Group Discussion and seven weeks of Personal Study. A leader guide is also provided to prepare those who are leading students through this journey.

FOR STUDENTS

Right away you will notice that this study might be different from other studies you've participated in. It is not designed for you to sit down and read from cover to cover. It is designed for you to study carefully, understand, and apply biblical principles to your life. It is about experiencing God, day by day, moment by moment.

To get the most out of this book, take your time by studying only one day at a time. Don't try to rush through several days at once. Try not to get behind and play catch-up by cramming a full week into one day. You need time to let the new information and ideas sink in. You are wanting to experience a person—Jesus. Time, focus, and meditation are the best way to allow the Holy Spirit to work in your life.

FOR LEADERS

Regardless of the day of the week your group meets, each week concludes with a group discussion to review the material from the four days of personal study and to unpack what students have been learning. This group time is designed to include video teaching and group discussion. Videos are available at lifeway.com/experiencinggod.

Each group study uses the following format to facilitate simple yet meaningful interaction among students with God's Word and the video teaching.

WATCH

Begin by watching the video teaching. The first week will serve as an introduction to the study. The videos that follow will expand on the material students have been learning in their personal study throughout the week. The following weeks will each cover one of the Seven Realities of Experiencing God.

DISCUSSION

Each week you will have an opportunity to discuss what students have learned in the video teaching and in the personal study days throughout the week. We've provided questions to help encourage discussion. Don't feel obligated to ask them all, and be open to discussing elements of the video or personal study not presented in the questions.

GOING DEEPER

This section includes Scripture, questions, and group activities that invite students to explore the content on a deeper level.

PREVIEW VIDEO

At the end of each group discussion, be sure to watch the preview video for the next week. This helps build anticipation and introduces students to the next reality that they will be exploring in the personal study days.

PRAYER AND DISMISSAL

Close each week with prayer. Take note of any prayer requests and ask students to give updates about how they've noticed God at work in their lives.

PERSONAL STUDY

Four days of personal study are provided each week to take students deeper into Scripture and to introduce the content that will be discussed in the Group Discussion. With Biblical teaching, interactive questions, relevant quotes, and creative activities, these sections challenge individuals to grow in their understanding of God's Word and will make the realities of experiencing God come alive.

LEADER GUIDE

At the back of this book, you'll find a Leader Guide that will help you prepare for each session. Use this guide to gain a broader understanding of the content and to learn ways you can engage with students at different levels of life-changing discussion.

HOW TO ACCESS THE VIDEOS

To stream the *Experiencing God* teen Bible study video teaching sessions, follow these steps:

1. Purchase the group video bundle at lifeway.com/experiencinggod.
2. Go to my.lifeway.com/redeem and register or log in to your Lifeway account.
3. Enter the redemption code provided at purchase to gain access to your group-use video license.

Once you've entered your personal redemption code, you can stream the video teaching sessions any time from your Digital Media page on my.lifeway.com or watch them via the Lifeway On Demand app on any TV or mobile device via your Lifeway account.

There's no need to enter your code more than once! To watch your streaming videos, just log in to your Lifeway account at my.lifeway.com or watch using the Lifeway On Demand app.

QUESTIONS? WE HAVE ANSWERS!

Visit support.lifeway.com and search "Video Redemption Code" or call our Tech Support Team at 866.627.8553.

INTRODUCTION TO
EXPERIENCING
GOD

In C. S. Lewis's book *The Voyage of the Dawn Treader*, three children are staring at an image of a ship at sea. The picture is unspectacular. It is just hanging on a wall, still and distant. Suddenly, it comes to life and the three characters are magically drawn into the frame. They are no longer staring at an inanimate portrait; they are inside it. They've gone from observers to characters in the story.

When you think about your faith, you may feel like the children staring at a picture. Perhaps it seems unspectacular and lifeless. God may feel distant. How do you go from being an observer of Christianity to an active participant in the rich world of faith you find in the Bible? You do so by experiencing God personally.

You might then ask the next logical question, "How do I experience God?" We're glad you asked. That's what this Bible study is all about.

Thirty years ago, our grandfather Henry Blackaby wrote *Experiencing God*. He developed it throughout years of walking with God in his own life and ministry. The truths in his book have impacted people across the world, from remote villages to professional sports teams to the White House. Now we want to help you discover those same timeless truths.

Experiencing God in your daily life is not something you observe from a distance; it requires participation. It's not a formula or an algorithm. God cannot be manipulated or predicted.

Take Moses. He spent the first forty years of his life in luxury, a Hebrew slave who was adopted into the royal family as a prince of Egypt. Then he killed a man and fled for his life into the wilderness.

Forty years later, God used a burning bush in the desert to get his attention. Unprepared and unqualified, Moses obeyed God and followed Him back to Egypt. The task God called Moses to do was too big for him to accomplish on his own. He could never be successful by staying on the outside. He had to be ready and willing to obey and follow God.

We're excited for you to join us on this journey. These next eight weeks can change your life. They can transform you from a passive observer in your faith into an active participant in the most exciting adventure of your life.

Are you ready to experience God? Let's jump into the picture and see what spectacular story God is unfolding.

WHILE YOU WATCH

As you watch the video, use the space provided to take notes or write down any thoughts and questions you may have.

DISCUSSION

Each week you will have an opportunity to discuss what you have learned from the video and in your personal study days. Spend time discussing the questions below as you prepare your hearts and minds to begin this Bible study.

What are the differences between knowing about something and experiencing something?

How would you describe the way your generation approaches religion, faith, and spirituality?

What about your family?

What about yourself?

What are some questions, doubts, or other obstacles that keep people from experiencing God?

What do you think keeps you from experiencing God?

What are some ways to overcome these obstacles?

What are you hoping to get out of this Bible study over the next eight weeks?

GOING DEEPER

As you begin this journey toward experiencing God, let's look at how several characters in the Bible began their own journeys following Jesus. John 1:35-42 tells the story about how Jesus called His first followers:

> *35 The next day again John was standing with two of his disciples, 36 and he looked at Jesus as he walked by and said, "Behold, the Lamb of God!" 37 The two disciples heard him say this, and they followed Jesus. 38 Jesus turned and saw them following and said to them, "What are you seeking?" And they said to him, "Rabbi" (which means Teacher), "where are you staying?" 39 He said to them, "Come and you will see." So they came and saw where he was staying, and they stayed with him that day, for it was about the tenth hour. 40 One of the two who heard John speak and followed Jesus was Andrew, Simon Peter's brother. 41 He first found his own brother Simon and said to him, "We have found the Messiah" (which means Christ). 42 He brought him to Jesus. Jesus looked at him and said, "You are Simon the son of John. You shall be called Cephas" (which means Peter).*

What stands out to you when you see how Jesus responded to the first two disciples that approached Him?

Why do you think Jesus told them to "come and see" rather than giving them a direct answer to their question?

Is it helpful for you to picture your personal faith as a journey you take with Jesus? Why or why not?

Continue reading the story below (John 1:43-51):

⁴³ The next day Jesus decided to go to Galilee. He found Philip and said to him, "Follow me." ⁴⁴ Now Philip was from Bethsaida, the city of Andrew and Peter. ⁴⁵ Philip found Nathanael and said to him, "We have found him of whom Moses in the Law and also the prophets wrote, Jesus of Nazareth, the son of Joseph." ⁴⁶ Nathanael said to him, "Can anything good come out of Nazareth?" Philip said to him, "Come and see." ⁴⁷ Jesus saw Nathanael coming toward him and said of him, "Behold, an Israelite indeed, in whom there is no deceit!" ⁴⁸ Nathanael said to him, "How do you know me?" Jesus answered him, "Before Philip called you, when you were under the fig tree, I saw you." ⁴⁹ Nathanael answered him, "Rabbi, you are the Son of God! You are the King of Israel!" ⁵⁰ Jesus answered him, "Because I said to you, 'I saw you under the fig tree,' do you believe? You will see greater things than these." ⁵¹ And he said to him, "Truly, truly, I say to you, you will see heaven opened, and the angels of God ascending and descending on the Son of Man."

What are some common themes or similarities you notice between the two Bible stories you just read?

Why do you think Philip told Nathanael to "come and see," rather than just explaining everything himself? Why might this be better for Nathanael?

What would it look like in your own life to "come and see" who Jesus is? If you are already a believer, what did it look like for you to "come and see" who Jesus is?

What are the benefits of going on a faith journey along with other people, like these first disciples did and like you will be doing with your group during this Bible study?

PREVIEW VIDEO

Watch the short preview video introducing *Reality 1: God is Always at Work Around You.*

PRAYER & DISMISSAL

As a group, share any prayer requests and spend time in prayer. You may want to write these requests below as a reminder to pray for the people in your group throughout the week.

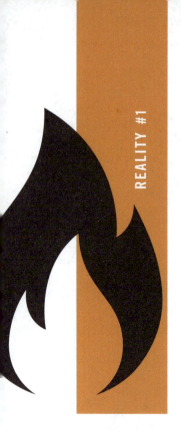

God Is Always at Work

Then Jacob awoke from his sleep and said, "Surely the LORD is in this place, and I did not know it."

GENESIS 28:16

Then Elisha prayed and said, "O LORD, please open his eyes that he may see." So the Lord opened the eyes of the young man, and he saw, and behold, the mountain was full of horses and chariots of fire all around Elisha.

2 KINGS 6:17

But Jesus answered them, "My Father is working until now, and I am working … Truly, truly, I say to you, the Son can do nothing of his own accord, but only what he sees the Father doing."

JOHN 5:17,19

PART OF A BIGGER PICTURE

As a teenager, I (Daniel) suffered from severe insomnia. I'd lay awake until almost five in the morning and would sometimes go three to four days without sleep. I tried everything. I was even examined by sleep doctors at professional clinics. Nothing helped.

Several years went by. I was exhausted, lonely, and confused. Didn't God love me? Didn't He want me to sleep? Couldn't I serve Him better if I was well-rested? One night at 3:00 a.m., I broke down and cried out to God, asking Him to reveal Himself and show me He hadn't forgotten me.

A few days later, I received a letter. A friend had written to encourage me and let me know that God loves me. I later discovered that on the same night I had prayed, she had awakened from a deep sleep and felt compelled to write to me—at exactly 3:00 a.m. Not only had God heard my prayer, but He was answering at the same time I was asking.

Her letter ended by wondering whether this was all part of a bigger picture that we couldn't see. Several months later at summer camp that picture was revealed a little more clearly. Our church gathered to share and pray and I asked everyone to pray for my insomnia. Right away, several people spoke up.

One guy had struggled with crippling depression all year. Early one morning he was preparing to commit suicide, but he decided to reach out to at least one person before he followed through. He called the only person he thought might still be awake at that hour—me. He concluded, "If Daniel hadn't been awake to answer my call, I would be dead today."

A sixteen-year-old girl shared next. Late at night, after a bad breakup, she had been consumed by suicidal thoughts. She needed to talk to someone, but who? Then she saw that, surprisingly, one person was still active in her online messenger. Me, again. She concluded, "Had Daniel not been online that night, I might not be alive today."

Several others shared similar stories. I had been focused on my own needs. I had prayed for God to do what I thought was best, and when He didn't, I wondered whether He was real or cared about me. That night at summer camp, I realized God had been at work all around me the entire time. His plans were far bigger than I could see at the time. I wanted better sleep; God wanted to save lives! God was at work, even when He seemed absent, and He wanted to include me. As we will see in the first reality of this Bible study, He wants to include you too.

Who Is God?

*"And this is eternal life, that they know you,
the only true God, and Jesus Christ whom you have sent."*

John 17:3

DAY 1

IS ANYBODY OUT THERE?

There is a scene in the film *The Avengers* where the Incredible Hulk grabs the villain Loki—a deity in both the Marvel Cinematic Universe and Norse mythology—and smashes him around like a toy doll. Afterward, with a laugh, the Hulk says, "Puny god!"[1] The idea that we, with all our scientific advancements, could replace God is not a new concept. In 1966, a now-famous *Time* magazine cover asked, "Is God Dead?" Many people believed that as society became more technologically advanced, we would leave God behind like an ancient artifact: something to admire from a previous historical age, but not necessary for the present.

Actor Daniel Radcliffe once said, "I'm an atheist, but I'm very relaxed about it. I don't preach my atheism, but I have a huge amount of respect for people [...] who do."[2] Radcliffe is most famous for starring in the Harry Potter films and seemed to be expressing a view that it might be fun to pretend to live in a magical world, but real life just isn't like that. He is not alone in how he feels.

Despite all of this skepticism, a general belief in God remains high in North America. In many parts of the world, Christianity is rapidly growing. How can there be both deep skepticism and growing faith happening in the world at the same?

What do you believe about God?

Ask yourself two crucial questions:

1. Does God exist?

2. If so, what kind of God is He?

FAITH DIAGNOSTICS

We encourage you to answer the questions throughout this book honestly. Don't worry about what you think the "right" answer is. Write down what you really think.

Let's begin by taking a quick diagnostic of what you do (or do not) believe:

1. On a scale of 1-5, how open are you to the possibility that there is a spiritual world beyond what you can see, taste, or touch?

    1   2   3   4   5

2. If there is something "out there," what do you think it's like?

3. On a scale of 1-5, how confident are you in what you currently believe?

    1   2   3   4   5

4. Do you live in a home where religion, faith, or spirituality is valued? Y/N If yes, how?

5. Do you wish your family was *more* or *less* religious or spiritual? Why?

6. What do you think this phrase means: "Spiritual but not religious." If this statement describes you, why?

A GOD-SHAPED HOLE

Belief in a God or gods is the human default. Cultures throughout history always started out religious and only later became atheistic (sometimes by force). What is it within us that desires to know a reality beyond what we experience every day?

Blaise Pascal was a famous scientist and philosopher who invented and built the first calculator in 1642 when he was just a teenager. He believed that each person has a God-shaped space in their heart that only He can fill, like the perfect piece to a puzzle.

In Romans 1:19-20, Paul said we can know some things about God simply by observing the world around us:

> [19] *For what can be known about God is plain to them, because God has shown it to them.* [20] *For his invisible attributes, namely, his eternal power and divine nature, have been clearly perceived, ever since the creation of the world, in the things that have been made. So they are without excuse.*

"At this moment it seems as though science will never be able to raise the curtain on the mystery of creation. For the scientist who has lived by his faith in the power of reason, the story ends like a bad dream. He has scaled the mountains of ignorance; he is about to conquer the highest peak; as he pulls himself over the final rock, he is greeted by a band of theologians who have been sitting there for centuries."[3]

—Robert Jastrow

"There is enough light for those who desire only to see, and enough darkness for those of a contrary position."[4]

—Blaise Pascal

If there is a God, and if He created the world, then what "clues" can you see in His creation that point to Him? List the first three that come to mind:

1. _____

2. _____

3. _____

Sometimes we encounter things that make us feel small in comparison, take our breath away, or inspire us to be a better person. Have you ever experienced a feeling like these? When was it?

WHO IS GOD?

The Bible is not simply a manual on "how to be a good person." Instead, it is largely the account of how God has revealed Himself to people in history. The biblical God is radically different from what other cultures believed about their gods. Genesis 11:1-9 tells the famous "Tower of Babel" story. This tower was likely a ziggurat, a tall, hollow building shaped like a stair-stepped pyramid. It was meant for gods to use as a stairway to descend from heaven to earth. It was empty inside except the room on top, which might contain a bed, food, and other items to entice a god to leave heaven and visit earth. But the God we read about in the Bible took the initiative and came to people without being summoned in any way.

God most fully revealed Himself in a personal way through Jesus in the New Testament. Colossians 1:15 tells us that Jesus was the "image of the invisible God." If nature gives us clues that God exists, then Jesus shows us more specifically who this God is. If you want to know what God is like, you should look to Jesus. Jesus Himself claimed, "Whoever has seen me has seen the Father" (John 14:9).

IN SUMMARY

- People are naturally religious or spiritual.
- Nature provides clues to God's existence.
- The God of the Bible is unique among the other religions of the world.
- Jesus reveals to us most clearly what God is like.

PREPARE FOR THE GROUP DISCUSSION

One thing that stood out to me today is:

One question I have based on today's study is:

CLOSING PRAYER

God, if You are there, please reveal Yourself to me this week. Help me to experience You as I pray and read verses from the Bible. Help me to have an open mind as I search for what is true.

God's Grand Narrative

I remember the days of old; I meditate on all that you have done; I ponder the work of your hands.

Psalm 143:5

A DIVINE DIRECTOR

I (Daniel) once toured the backlot of Warner Brothers Studios. It was amazing to see the different sound stages, props, and sets that were used to create so many great movies. The highlight came when I glanced across the lunchroom to see director Christopher Nolan (*Dark Knight* trilogy, *Inception*, *Tenet*) eating just a few tables away.

A skilled movie director has a vision for a story and the ability to oversee the cast and crew to fulfill it. A blockbuster film requires as many as three thousand crew members all working together to achieve the director's goals.

God is like a director of a massive story playing out on a universal scale throughout history. He created the world with the intention that humanity would live in harmony with each other and their Creator. But humanity rebelled against their Creator, desiring to sit in the director's chair (see Gen. 3). Here's the good news: God did not abandon His creative project! The Bible tells us how God has been drawing people back to Himself, all leading up to Jesus—the hero of the whole story. Jesus's death paid the penalty for our rebellion and His resurrection means the end of the story is one of hope. Ultimately, His sacrifice brings us back into a right relationship with God.

BIBLICAL STORYBOARDING

Part of the process of making a movie is creating a "storyboard," sketches that demonstrate how the whole story fits together from start to finish. We've listed some of the big "scenes" in the biblical story. In the space provided on page 22, sketch out a simple storyboard for three to five of the scenes listed. Pick the ones that stand out to you the most. Don't worry if you're not a great artist!

1 God creates the universe (Gen. 1–2).

2 Humanity rebels against God (Gen. 3).

3 God judges humans using a flood, but saves Noah's family in an ark (Gen. 6–9).

4 God reveals himself to Abram and promises to make his family a great nation (Gen. 12:1-9).

5 Abram's ancestors become slaves in Egypt. God hears their cries and, in the form of a burning bush, calls Moses (Ex. 3).

6 God does miracles through Moses to rescue His people and parts the waters of the Red Sea bringing His people through safely (Ex. 7–14).

7 God delivers the Ten Commandments as laws for His people (Ex. 20:1-20).

8 Joshua leads the people into the promised land and conquerors the city of Jericho by marching around it seven times (Joshua 1–7).

9 God chooses a teenage shepherd named David to become king, and his faith leads him to defeat a giant (1 Sam. 16–17).

10 David's son Solomon builds a great temple to worship God (1 Kings 6).

11 God's people are defeated by the nations of Assyria, then Babylon, and many of them are taken captive to these foreign lands (2 Kings 17; 25).

12 God sends an angel to a young girl named Mary to tell her that she will give birth to the Son of God (Luke 1:26-38).

13 At the age of 30, Jesus gathers twelve disciples and spends three years healing and teaching (Matt.; Mark; Luke; John).

14 Jesus is crucified on a cross but is miraculously raised from the dead three days later (Matt. 27–28; Mark 15–16; Luke 23–24; John 18–20).

15 The disciples take the message of Jesus (the gospel) around the world (Acts).

"Literally everything in the Bible is about [Jesus]. The Bible can only be understood if it is seen to be about him."[1]

—Timothy Keller

Take a look at your artistry! Can you see how God has been telling one big story throughout history? Based on these scenes and pictures, what major themes do you see?

In what ways does the whole story fit together and point towards a single goal?

GOD'S WILL

All of these stories ultimately point to Jesus (John 5:39; Luke 24:27). Jesus knew His place in God's great story: "For I have come down from heaven, not to do my will, but the will of him who sent me" (John 6:38). Jesus's purpose was to accomplish His heavenly Father's will. The word "will" means the desires and goals that direct someone's actions.

What was God's will? Jesus tells us that too: "For this is the will of my Father, that everyone who looks on the Son and believes in him should have eternal life, and I will raise him up on the last day" (John 6:40). God's will is to bring people back into a relationship with Himself.

We often start with the question, "What is God's will for me?" rather than simply, "What is God's will?" Unlike Jesus, we tend to make it all about us rather than all about God. This self-centeredness can cause us to miss what God is doing. It also fails to acknowledge God as the director. Your personal story is important, but it is also part of a bigger story that stretches all the way back to the beginning of time. God is the director of the greatest story ever told, and it is still unfolding all around you.

Do you see yourself as having a role in God's story? Why or why not?

IN SUMMARY

- God has been active throughout all of history.
- The stories in the Bible all point to Jesus.
- Your life is part of a much bigger story that began at creation and continues today.
- God's will is to bring people back into a relationship with Himself.

PREPARE FOR THE GROUP DISCUSSION

One thing that stood out to me today is:

One question I have based on today's study is:

CLOSING PRAYER

Thank you, God, for the amazing story You have been directing since the beginning of time. Open my eyes to see this story unfolding around me this week.

Characters In a Story

"...where have you come from and where are you going?"

Genesis 16:8

STORIES AND STORYTELLERS

Humans are naturally drawn to stories. From the ancient cave drawings to the latest hit novels and movies, we've been telling stories for thousands of years. Stories give people something in common, and they have allowed us to come together to accomplish more than any other species on the planet.[5] In fact, even when we go to sleep, our brains continue to tell us stories.

If you had to describe the Bible in just two or three words, what would they be?

You may have heard the acronym: Basic Instruction Before Leaving Earth. But the Bible is far more than just a dull instruction manual. It's a thrilling drama filled with dynamic characters, shocking plot twists, and page-turning adventures!

Did you know that more than sixty-percent of the Bible is written in the form of narrative or story? Jesus was a storyteller. The Bible says that when Jesus spoke to the crowds, "he said nothing to them without a parable" (Matt. 13:34).

Why do you think God gave us the Bible predominantly in the form of stories instead of a long list of "dos" and "don'ts"?

An instruction manual can tell you what to do (or not do). It provides information. A story allows you to experience something. We are created to view the world in terms of a story because God did not intend for us simply to learn about life, but to experience it.

When you read the stories in the Bible, you are reading earlier chapters of a bigger narrative. And guess what? The narrative is not over. You are a character living out the later chapters of that same story.

NOT JUST AN OBSERVER

Are you familiar with a man in the Bible called Zacchaeus? This is his story:

> [1] "He [Jesus] entered Jericho and was passing through. [2] There was a man named Zacchaeus who was a chief tax collector, and he was rich. [3] He was trying to see who Jesus was, but he was not able because of the crowd, since he was a short man. [4] So running ahead, he climbed up a sycamore tree to see Jesus, since he was about to pass that way. [5] When Jesus came to the place, he looked up and said to him, "Zacchaeus, hurry and come down because today it is necessary for me to stay at your house." [6] So he quickly came down and welcomed him joyfully. [7] All who saw it began to complain, "He's gone to stay with a sinful man." [8] But Zacchaeus stood there and said to the Lord, "Look, I'll give half of my possessions to the poor, Lord. And if I have extorted anything from anyone, I'll pay back four times as much." [9] "Today salvation has come to this house," Jesus told him, "because he too is a son of Abraham. [10] For the Son of Man has come to seek and to save the lost."

Luke 19:1-10 (CSB)

Where is Zacchaeus at the start of this story and what is his goal?

Why do you think he made such an effort to see Jesus?

What questions do you think went through his head when he heard Jesus call his name?

Psychologists have conducted studies showing the benefit of understanding your life as a unified story. This principle is particularly evident when we experience pain or trauma. They found that those who could write out and understand painful experiences within the context of their life story actually experienced better physical health up to a year later.[6]

"You are perfectly cast in your life. I can't imagine anyone but you in the role. Go play."[7]

—Lin-Manuel Miranda

Circle the emotions below that you might have felt if you were in Zacchaeus's position (you can choose more than one):

Excited   Terrified   Confused   Angry

Panicked   Curious   Other _____

How does Zacchaeus change by the end of the story?

Zacchaeus had heard about Jesus. Many of the rumors circulating—miraculous deeds, supernatural healings, casting out demons—would have been hard to believe, but they were enough to compel Zacchaeus to climb a tree just to catch a glimpse of this interesting man. When he went up the tree, he was just an observer; when he came down, he was a participant.

CALLED TO JOIN GOD'S STORY

Mike's friend Brad was once given tickets to see his favorite band. Halfway through the concert, the band always invited a musician from the audience to come on stage and play guitar with them for the next song, and they chose Brad. He went from being an observer to a participant and discovered that those are completely different experiences!

We asked how you would feel to be in Zacchaeus's place. The truth is that you are in his place. No, you're probably not sitting in a tree right now, but just like Zacchaeus, God doesn't want you to be a passive observer. God's story is happening all around you.

Are you ready to climb down the tree and be part of it?

IN SUMMARY

- Humans are naturally drawn to stories.
- Jesus taught primarily using stories.
- We are all characters in a bigger story God is creating.
- God wants us to be active participants, not just passive observers, in His story.

PREPARE FOR THE GROUP DISCUSSION

One thing that stood out to me today is:

One question I have based on today's study is:

CLOSING PRAYER

God, please open my eyes to Your story all around me. Show me how I fit into that story so that I might be an active participant, not just a passive observer.

God's Story and Your Story

For we are God's masterpiece. He has created us anew in Christ Jesus, so we can do the good things he planned for us long ago.

Ephesians 2:10

THE IMPORTANCE OF PERSPECTIVE

Michelangelo's *David* is perhaps the most famous sculpture ever made. However, if you visit the gallery in Florence, Italy, where it is displayed, you might notice something shocking. It's flawed! The proportions are off. The head and upper body are too large. Is Michelangelo overrated?

Actually, the sculpture was originally created to be displayed along the roof of the Florence Cathedral. When viewers looked up at the sculpture, the proportions would appear correct. Far from being a mistake, the enlarged proportions actually show Michelangelo's true genius. The problem is not with the artwork but the location. It is not positioned where it was created to be.

Earlier this week we spoke of God being a master storyteller. Yesterday you learned the amazing truth that you are called to be an active character in that story. Just like *David*, God has created you for a specific place, so that when people look at your life, they will be amazed by the One who created you (Matt. 5:16).

UNFINISHED MASTERPIECES

Ephesians 2:10 (NLT) says, "For we are God's masterpiece. He has created us anew in Christ Jesus, so we can do the good things he planned for us long ago."

Do you feel like a masterpiece? In the left-hand column, list the ways you do feel like a masterpiece. In the right column, list the reasons you do not:

I Do   I Do Not

According to Ephesians 2:10, what is your purpose?

You are a masterpiece, but an unfinished masterpiece. Hebrews 10:14 (NIV) says, "For by one sacrifice he has made perfect forever those who are being made holy." God made you a masterpiece, but He is not finished yet! As you live out God's purposes for you, He will continue to grow your character throughout your entire life. One day, when we come to live with God in heaven, He will complete everything He started in us (Phil. 1:6).

COMPETING STORIES

The message we often get from western culture is that you should be the author of your own story. Most video games today offer a staggering number of customization options and gameplay flexibility, so that the gaming experience can be fine-tuned to the player's exact preferences.

The Bible offers a different perspective.

> "The one who loves his life will lose it, and the one who hates his life in this world will keep it for eternal life" (John 12:25, CSB).

What does Jesus mean when He says a person should "hate" his life?

> "I am the Lord your God, who brought you up out of Egypt. Open wide your mouth and I will fill it. But my people would not listen to me; Israel would not submit to me. So I gave them over to their stubborn hearts to follow their own devices" (Ps. 81:10-12, NIV).

What is the consequence of choosing our own story instead of God's?

> "Well done, good and faithful servant! You have been faithful with a few things; I will put you in charge of many things. Come and share your master's happiness!" (Matt. 25:21, NIV).

What is the reward for choosing God's story over ours?

WHAT SORT OF TALE HAVE YOU FALLEN INTO?

There is a wonderful moment in *The Lord of the Rings* when heroes Frodo and Sam, two small Hobbits, reflect on their circumstances:

> "The brave things in the old tales and songs, . . . the tales that really mattered, or the ones that stay in the mind. Folk seem to have been just landed in them. . . . I expect they had lots of chances, like us, of turning back, only they didn't. And if they had, we shouldn't know, because they'd have been forgotten. We hear about those as just went on, and not all to a good end, mind you; at least not to what folk inside a story and not outside it call a good end. . . . I wonder what sort of a tale we've fallen into?"[8]

Their tale would be difficult, challenging, exciting, terrifying, and everything in between. Later, as the two Hobbits rest on the side of Mount Doom, the evil ring destroyed and their adventure coming to an end, Sam sighs, "What a tale we have been in, Mr. Frodo, haven't we?"[9]

What sort of tale have you fallen into? Will you press on or turn back? Revelation 20:11-13 describes a "book of life" in heaven that contains the works and deeds of your life. What sort of story will it tell?

IN SUMMARY

- We are each an "unfinished masterpiece."
- God has planned "good works" for each of us.
- We are each writing a story with our lives.
- We have a choice to accept or reject God's story for us.

PREPARE FOR THE GROUP DISCUSSION

One thing that stood out to me today is:

One question I have based on today's study is:

CLOSING PRAYER

Thank You, God, for including me in the bigger story You are telling. Thank You for the good works You have planned for me to accomplish. Help me to choose Your story for my life this week.

WHILE YOU WATCH

As you watch the video, use the space provided to take notes or write down any thoughts and questions you may have.

DISCUSSION

Based on what you learned in the video and in your personal Bible study days throughout the week, spend time discussing the questions below.

Mike and Daniel describe Christianity as being a character in the exciting story that God—the Divine Director—has been telling since the beginning of time.

Why do we, as humans, connect so much with stories?

What are some reasons why God might have chosen to give us the Bible as a book of many stories, rather than a more straightforward instruction manual for life or a theology textbook?

Have you ever thought of your life as part of a bigger story? Why is it sometimes difficult to see the bigger picture beyond our immediate circumstances?

On page 22 you drew out a "storyboard" for the unified narrative of the Bible. Which stories in the Bible do you relate to most? Why?

At the beginning of the week Daniel shared about his insomnia (page 15). Why can it be so difficult to see God when we are hurting?

Has God ever worked in your life in ways that surprised you or didn't fully make sense at the time? Can you share an example?

At the end of each day this week you wrote down one main takeaway and one question you had. Take turns sharing one of your takeaways or questions with the group.

GOING DEEPER

For many people today, Christianity is seen as a myth or fantasy. People of faith can even be mocked or made to feel foolish for believing that what the Bible teaches is actually true.

Have you ever been made to feel this way? What was your response?

If this God doesn't exist, or if He is not at work in the world, how would this change your outlook on life?

If a loving God does exist, and if He is working in the world, how should this affect the way you look at life?

Christianity is an exciting story, but it's not just a story. The reason the gospel is called the "good news" is because it's a true story. The apostle Paul even saw clues in nature that pointed to the truth of the Christian story. Read Romans 1:19-20:

> *19 For what can be known about God is plain to them, because God has shown it to them. 20 For his invisible attributes, namely, his eternal power and divine nature, have been clearly perceived, ever since the creation of the world, in the things that have been made. So they are without excuse.*

What clues do you see in nature that point to God?

What might God's creation tell us about His personality and character?

What are the limitations of learning about God through nature (what can't it tell us about God)?

The disciple Peter understood that people would be skeptical about the story of Jesus. People back then, just like people today, did not want to just believe anything. They wanted to have good reasons to believe. Read what Peter wrote in 2 Peter 1:16-21 (CSB):

> *16 For we did not follow cleverly contrived myths when we made known to you the power and coming of our Lord Jesus Christ; instead, we were eyewitnesses of his majesty. 17 For he received honor and glory from God the Father when the voice came to him from the Majestic Glory, saying "This is my beloved Son, with whom I am well-pleased!" 18 We ourselves heard this voice when it came from heaven while we were with him on the holy mountain. 19 We also have the prophetic word strongly confirmed, and you will do well to pay attention to it, as to a lamp shining in a dark place, until the day dawns and the morning star rises in your hearts. 20 Above all, you know this: No prophecy of Scripture comes from the prophet's own interpretation, 21 because no prophecy ever came by the will of man; instead, men spoke from God as they were carried along by the Holy Spirit.*

How could Peter share the story of Jesus with such confidence?

Peter claimed that the prophecies in Scripture were not made-up by people, but were actually inspired by the Holy Spirit. How should this affect the way we read the Bible?

How do these verses give you confidence in your own faith to share the story of Jesus with other people?

PREVIEW VIDEO

Watch the short video introducing *Reality 2: God Pursues*.

PRAYER & DISMISSAL

As a group, share any prayer requests and spend time in prayer. You may want to write these requests below as a reminder to pray for the people in your group throughout the week.

God Pursues

I have loved you, my people, with an everlasting love. With unfailing love I have drawn you to myself.

JEREMIAH 31:3 (NLT)

"For God so loved the world, that he gave his only Son, that whoever believes in him should not perish but have eternal life."

JOHN 3:16

Now we have received not the spirit of the world, but the Spirit who is from God, that we might understand the things freely given us by God.

1 CORINTHIANS 2:12

"Behold, I stand at the door and knock. If anyone hears my voice and opens the door, I will come in to him and eat with him, and he with me."

REVELATION 3:20

LOVE, X-RAYS, AND A BABY GIRAFFE

I (Mike) remember when I asked Sarah to marry me. We were visiting my parents in South Carolina for Christmas, and I managed to sneak out and purchase a ring. Everything was coming together perfectly, and then I got sick. Really sick. I spent most of the holidays as a miserable blob stuck to my parents' couch. As the days ticked by, I realized I was running out of time.

My Perfect Plan: Enjoy a romantic dinner downtown and then take a walk in a park that has a beautiful waterfall. As we gaze into each other's eyes, I fall to one knee and utter the words she has been waiting for her entire life: "How would you like all your dreams to come true? Will you marry me?" She whispers, through tears of joy, "Yes." We embrace. Birds sing. Fireworks explode. Strangers applaud. The whole thing was just magical, in my mind.

How It Actually Happened: "Mike," Sarah said, "You're too sick to leave this house unless you get permission from a doctor." I reminded her that my dad had a PhD (in history), so that technically made him a doctor. He said I was fine! "No, I mean a real doctor." Uh, oh.

As I dragged my feeble body into the examination room of the local walk-in medical clinic, I pleaded with the doctor on call. "Please, you have to tell my girlfriend that I am healthy enough to go downtown! I plan to ask her to marry me!" The doctor, moved by my desperation and likely breaking her Hippocratic oath to "do no harm," gave me the all clear. I still don't know what my x-rays actually said, but evidently it wasn't fatal. So, off we went!

The only way I could convince Sarah to go to the park was if I promised to take her to the zoo afterwards to see the new baby giraffe. As we meandered down the path, I desperately looked for a place to propose, but all the best spots were taken. Time dragged on. The zoo closed. I had second thoughts about what Sarah's answer would be. That is, if I ever actually got the chance to ask her!

Then I saw it. At the end of the path was a quiet stream and a rock big enough for two. We sat down, and I mustered enough inner strength to pop the question. She said "Yes!" The best part was she still got to see the baby giraffe—the next day, when the zoo reopened.

Love can make us do crazy things. It can drive us forward no matter what obstacles (or sicknesses) threaten to hold us back. Love is active. It pursues.

This week, we are going to look at God's love for you. We will find that nothing, not even sin and death, will stand in the way of God pursuing a relationship with you.

God Pursues

I have loved you, my people, with an everlasting love.
With unfailing love I have drawn you to myself.

Jeremiah 31:3 (NLT)

DAY 1

STUMBLING AROUND BLIND

Daniel staggered out of the eye doctor's office with dilated eyes. The world was a blur. His wife was shopping nearby and awaiting a text message to come pick him up. Despite foggy vision, he managed to open his messages and (with the help of auto-correct) send, "I'm done." With eyes too blind to read the response messages and getting impatient, Daniel just kept typing, "I'm done" over and over. Hours later, when his eyes began to clear, he eventually realized the problem. He hadn't been texting his wife. He had been messaging a co-worker! The concerned co-worker was panicking, worried that Daniel had snapped and decided to quit his job or something worse, and needed immediate intervention.

According to the Bible, we are blinded by our sin (1 John 2:11; 2 Cor. 4:3-4; Matt. 13:10-17). We all suffer the same condition and cannot connect to God on our own, no matter how hard we try.

> *10 There is no one righteous, not even one. 11 There is no one who understands; there is no one who seeks God. 12 All have turned away; all alike have become worthless. There is no one who does what is good, not even one.*

Romans 3:10-12 (CSB)

Yikes! These versus paint a bleak picture. We can't do enough good to reach God. In fact, on our own, we don't even know what good is. This is a hopeless feeling.

Describe a time when you felt like you were not "good enough" (as a Christian, at school, in your family, on a sports team, etc.):

What were three emotions you felt during the experience described above?

Whether we realize it or not, we can easily fall into the belief that Christianity is all about doing good things and not doing bad things. Perhaps you've felt guilty for not living the way you were "supposed" to live. Like being trapped in sinking sand, the harder we try the more we sink, always feeling like we have done too much bad and not enough good.

Here's the good news: you don't need to chase after God as if He were running from you. Actually, the opposite is true. He is the one who chases us. This week we will look at *Reality 2: God pursues a continuing love relationship with you that is real and personal.* Over the next few days we'll focus on each part of this amazing truth.

IN PURSUIT

What does it mean to pursue something? It involves setting a specific goal—athletic excellence, high grades, a promotion at your job, and so on—and then working to achieve it. Studies have shown that often those who achieve at a high level are not those who are smarter or more talented; it is those who pursue their goals with passion, hard work, and consistency.[1]

What are some goals you've pursued in your life?

Did you achieve your goal? If so, how hard did you work to achieve it?

When we are passionate about a goal, we will do whatever it takes to achieve it. If we will do this for our goals, how much more will God pursue His goals? He desires to be in a relationship with you, but sin prevents you from ever finding or working your way to Him. So, God pursues you.

"For God so loved the world, that he gave his only Son, that whoever believes in him should not perish but have eternal life."

John 3:16

"Knowing God without knowing our own wretchedness makes for pride. Knowing our own wretchedness without knowing God makes for despair. Knowing Jesus Christ strikes the balance because he shows us both God and our own wretchedness."[2]

—Blaise Pascal

Jesus—the only perfect person—is the answer to our hopeless problem of never being "good enough." But God did not stop there. Ever since, He has been actively and relentlessly drawing people toward Jesus, like someone guiding a blind person to an eye doctor able to restore their sight:

> *"No one can come to me unless the Father who sent me draws them, and I will raise them up at the last day"*
>
> **John 6:44 (NIV)**

If the Bible says that you can't seek God on our own, but you are currently reading a book about knowing God, what does that mean? It means God is at work pursuing you right now, drawing you to Himself. If He wasn't working, then you wouldn't be reading this book.

REFLECTIVE JOURNALING

Let's end today with some reflective journaling. The purpose of this activity is not to come up with well-thought-out, polished answers. We want you to think with your pen. Use the prompts below, and write whatever comes to mind.

Sometimes I feel like I'm not worthy of God's love because...

Knowing that I don't need to chase after God because God pursues me is...

Because God takes the initiative to relentlessly pursue me, I desire to...

IN SUMMARY

- Sin blinds us so we cannot find God on our own.
- God pursues a relationship with us.
- We pursue the things we are passionate about.
- We don't have to earn God's love by our good actions because He already loves us.

PREPARE FOR THE GROUP DISCUSSION

One thing that stood out to me today is:

One question I have based on today's study is:

CLOSING PRAYER

Thank You, God, for pursuing me even when I wasn't looking for You. Please help me to remember this truth during the upcoming week and live my life in response to it.

Love

Love is patient and kind; love does not envy or boast; it is not arrogant or rude. It does not insist on its own way; it is not irritable or resentful; it does not rejoice at wrongdoing, but rejoices with the truth. Love bears all things, believes all things, hopes all things, endures all things. Love never ends.

1 Corinthians 13:4-8

DAY 2

COUNTERFEIT

Joyce Hatto was an aspiring pianist living in London, but her dreams fizzled out. When illness forced an early retirement, she passed the time by recording herself playing classical compositions and releasing them on a small record label run by her husband. To the astonishment of music critics, the songs were excellent! She recorded over 120 albums and earned worldwide acclaim. When she died, *The Guardian* proclaimed her as "one of the greatest pianists Britain has ever produced."[3]

Hatto's inspiring underdog story took a turn when one listener noticed that one of her songs sounded similar to a recording by another pianist. A little too similar. Joyce Hatto was not a prodigy artist—she was a con artist! Every song had been stolen from lesser known musicians, altered with clever sound engineering, and sold to listeners who couldn't tell the difference.

Unless you know the real thing, it's easy to be duped by counterfeits. The Bible tells us that God loves us. But how do we know that we're experiencing this real love and not just a counterfeit version?

WHAT IS LOVE?

People use the word "love" to describe a lot of different things. Here are some of ours: peanut butter (Mike), heavy metal (Daniel), our wives (both), geeky fantasy novels (Daniel), drums (Mike), ketchup chips (both, it's a Canadian thing…), and Star Wars (both).

What are some things you've used the word "love" to describe?

When we use a term so broadly, it can start to lose its meaning. When love describes how we feel about junk food, video games, and face-melting guitar solos, it cheapens the word when it comes to bigger ideas like this one: "This is real love—not that we loved God, but that he loved us and sent his Son as a sacrifice to take away our sins" (1 John 4:10, NLT).

Jesus sometimes spoke of the "world" to refer to the mindset and values that run contrary to God's character and will. He prayed that His disciples would be "in the world" but not like the world (John 17:14-19). We can often see this contrast in the entertainment industry. Think of your favorite show, movie, book, or some piece of celebrity gossip you've recently seen on social media and then answer the following questions:

What image of love do these things present?

Complete this sentence: The three words that best sum up how pop culture typically thinks about love are _____, _____, and _____.

Here are three words that we came up with:

- Love is a **feeling**: Butterflies in the stomach or burning lust and attraction. Disney has made countless movies in which the main character is encouraged to follow his or her heart. But feelings come and go; they can change quickly. In fact, sometimes our feelings can even fool us. Jeremiah 17:9 says, "The heart is deceitful above all things, and desperately sick; who can understand it?"

- Love is **temporary**: If people can "fall in" love, then they can also "fall out" of love. Falling also gives the impression of something you have little control over.

- Love is **conditional**: When our emotional or physical needs are no longer met, we exchange one object of love for another, like a football team cutting an underperforming quarterback for a rookie. This view of love puts the focus on us, not them. It's selfish.

GOD'S PERFECT LOVE

It's been said that bankers learn to spot counterfeit bills not by examining forged bills but by becoming intimately familiar with the real thing.

Don't measure God's love by the standards of the culture around you; use God's love as the ultimate standard to measure all others. God's character is the foundation of His love (1 John 4:16). We shouldn't define love on our own terms and then expect God to fit into our definition. Rather, we should examine our ideas on love and make sure they line up with who God is.

Also, we want to clarify that a "love relationship" is not the same thing as a "romantic relationship." Sometimes the language we use in church (especially in the songs we sing) can make it sound like Jesus is our significant other. However, "love" can describe many sorts of deep relationships (parent/child, student/teacher, player/coach, best friends) that are not romantic.

Here are three essential truths to keep in mind about God's love.

1. God's love is who He is.

God displays love in His actions because that is who He is. Our nature directs what we do, and what we do reveals who we are. (See 1 John 4:8,16.)

"Anyone who does not love does not know God, because God is love. . . . So we have come to know and to believe the love that God has for us. God is love, and whoever abides in love abides in God, and God abides in him."

1 John 4:8,16

"But God demonstrates his own love for us in this: While we were still sinners, Christ died for us."

Romans 5:8

"This is how God showed his love among us: He sent his one and only Son into the world that we might live through him. This is love: not that we loved God, but that he loved us and sent his Son as an atoning sacrifice for our sins."

1 John 4:9-11

"Give thanks to the God in heaven. His love endures forever."

Psalm 136:26

2. God's love is unconditional.

Have you ever felt like you did not deserve to be loved because of the bad things you've done? God's love is not based on what we deserve or have earned. In fact, God loves us even at our most unlovable. (See Rom. 5:8 and 1 John 4:9-11.)

3. God's love lasts forever.

Have you been afraid of losing love once you've found it? Do you fear being abandoned by those who claim to love you? God's love for us is unconditional and doesn't end. (See Ps. 136:26.)

TRUE LOVE VS. IMITATION LOVE

In order to fully appreciate what it means for God to pursue a love relationship with you, you must distinguish between God's authentic love and anything else that advertises itself as love, but does not reflect God's character. To compare the two different loves, choose one (or more) of the ideas below.

Write or find a short poem (we are talking about love, after all), create visual art, compare song lyrics (or write your own), write out a definition for each, make a list of examples, think of a story (or write your own), or write down a memory that includes a time when you experienced each type of love.

God's Love   Counterfeit Love

IN SUMMARY

- We use the word "love" to describe many things, but this broad definition can confuse our understanding of what love is.
- God's character is the foundation for love.
- The culture around us sometimes presents a counterfeit love that does not reflect God's character.
- God's love for you is perfect, unearned, and lasts forever.

PREPARE FOR THE GROUP DISCUSSION

One thing that stood out to me today is:

One question I have based on today's study is:

CLOSING PRAYER

God, thank You for loving me with a perfect love. Please give me wisdom to see the difference between true love and counterfeit love. Help me to love others with a love that shows them what You are like.

Relationship

"Behold, I stand at the door and knock. If anyone hears my voice and opens the door, I will come in to him and eat with him, and he with me."

Revelation 3:20

AN UNEXPECTED GUEST

As a teenager, I (Mike) worked at a Canadian coffee shop called Tim Hortons. Not much exciting ever happened in our little town, but one day the beloved coach of our nearby National Hockey League team came in for lunch. I freaked out (to put it mildly). In my excitement, I kept tripping over myself and completely messed up his order. On his way out, I blurted, "Can I have your autograph!?" He waited patiently as I frantically turned the kitchen upside down until I found a pen and a take-out sandwich bag for him to sign. He may not remember me, but I'll never forget him!

CELEBRITY OR FRIEND?

Mike's embarrassing experience is actually not far off from how many people view God—He is like a celebrity we admire from afar. We know about Him, but we don't really know Him (and He doesn't care to know us). But the Bible doesn't describe God that way. The hockey coach in Mike's story came into the restaurant to eat by himself, but Revelation 3:20 paints a picture of Jesus wanting to come in and eat with His people. Sharing a meal with someone has been considered a sign of trust and friendship in many cultures throughout history.

In John 17:3, Jesus said, "...this is eternal life, that they know you, the only true God, and Jesus Christ whom you have sent." When Jesus talked about "knowing" God, He was not referring to head knowledge; He was speaking about a relationship. For that reason, the Bible doesn't spend much time addressing atheism. Even the demons believe that God exists (James 2:19). Between the two of us, we have five young sons and one daughter. It is our sincere hope that they don't just grow up to believe we exist, but that they will long for a deep relationship with us. If we feel this way about our own kids, how much more must God desire a relationship with His children (Matt. 7:11)?

CREATED FOR RELATIONSHIPS

We were created for relationships. Healthy relationships are important for our social well-being, and they also affect our physical health. A strong connection to community makes us less likely to experience colds, heart attacks, strokes, cancer, depression, and even premature death![4]

Why do you think relationships are so important?

Describe your closest relationship (a friend, a parent, a sibling, etc.). What makes this relationship special to you?

Describe a time in your life when you felt alone or abandoned. Why was it so difficult?

Developing healthy relationships can take hard work. Based on your own experience in relationships (the good and bad), complete the two lists below:

The five most important things for a healthy relationship are:

1

2

3

4

5

The five most harmful things for a relationship are:

1

2

3

4

5

When the COVID-19 crisis hit in 2020 and people suddenly had to stay home, online video platforms were flooded because everyone tried to find ways to stay connected in their relationships. In fact, Zoom skyrocketed from a daily global usage peak of 10 million people to more than 200 million![5]

Do you see how the things you listed might help or hurt your relationship with God, just as they do your relationships with other people? Like any other relationship, your relationship with God will grow as you spend more time together.

HEAVENLY FATHER

One way that the Bible describes God's relationship with us is as a "heavenly Father" (Matt. 6:9). Actually, God is referred to as "Father" about 172 times in the four gospels.[6] This metaphor can be difficult to understand for people who have had an absent or strained relationship with their earthly father.

> What kind of relationship do you have with your earthly father?

> How might this relationship, good or bad, influence your view of God as your heavenly Father?

It's tempting to judge God based on the good or bad example our earthly father set. But the Bible uses the Aramaic word "Abba" to describe God (Rom. 8:15). That word was the most intimate term children could use for their dad. Psalm 68:5 describes God as a "father of the fatherless." In John 1:12 we read, "...to all who did receive [Jesus], who believed in his name, he gave the right to become children of God." No matter what kind of father or family you have, if you've placed your faith in Jesus, you have also been adopted into God's family, and He is a perfect and loving Father.

> How is your relationship with your heavenly Father?

Many of the most famous and vocal atheists in history had absent or abusive fathers. The comedian George Carlin expressed a common feeling when he said he didn't want to be "… just another religious robot, mindlessly and aimlessly and blindly believing that all of this is in the hands of some spooky incompetent father figure who doesn't [care]."[4] Carlin's mother left his alcoholic father when George was just two months old.

"God is not the reflection of your earthly dad. He is the perfection of your earthly dad."[5]

—Louie Giglio

IN SUMMARY

- We are social beings created for relationships.
- God does not just love you from afar; He desires a personal relationship with you.
- Relationships take time and effort to grow.
- God is our perfect heavenly Father.

PREPARING FOR THE GROUP DISCUSSION

One thing that stood out to me today is:

One question I have based on today's study is:

CLOSING PRAYER

Thank You, God, for being my perfect heavenly Father. Thank You that You will never leave or forsake me. Please draw me closer in relationship to You this week.

Your Most Important Relationship

Jesus answered, "The most important is Listen, Israel! The Lord our God, the Lord is one. Love the Lord your God with all your heart, with all your soul, with all your mind, and with all your strength. The second is, Love your neighbor as yourself. There is no other command greater than these."

Mark 12:29-31 (CSB)

PRICELESS

An elderly woman in France had a painting hanging in her kitchen for years. She believed it was just an old religious image with little value. When it came time to move out of her home, she brought in an auctioneer to help sell the furniture she no longer needed. He noticed the painting and had art experts investigate. Guess what they discovered? The painting was a rare thirteenth-century work by the artist Cimabue. It set a new record when it sold for almost $27 million! The woman had no idea that a priceless work of art had been hanging above her stove all those years.[7]

If that lady had realized sooner that she possessed something of such value, she could have lived a very different life. Do you see the value of the God of the universe wanting to be in relationship with you? Or is it something that may get overlooked in your everyday routines? Today we will look at how your relationship with God is the most valuable thing in your whole life.

THE BIG TWO

When you need help making a big decision or getting out of a difficult situation, who (or what) do you go to for help?

We had a friend who was struggling with some difficult circumstances. After she shared with us all she had done to try and fix her situation—getting advice from parents and friends, implementing suggestions from popular blogs, meeting with a mentor figure, practicing exercises her yoga instructor gave her—she concluded, "I guess all I can do now is pray." She had a relationship with God, but she was treating it as a last resort when everything else failed. She didn't realize the true value of what was right in front of her!

Your relationship with God is more important than any other relationship you have in your life. Do you treat it that way?

Look at the quote from Jesus at the top of this page. Some religious experts had asked Him a tough question: "Which commandment is the most important of all?" (Mark 12:28). They were trying to trap Him. Surely all the commandments were equally important? Jesus answered them with two: First, love God with all your soul, mind, and strength. And second, love your neighbor as yourself (Mark 12:29-31).

Why do you think Jesus chose these two commandments?

Why do you think Jesus said to love God first and then to love your neighbor second?

Does it seem strange to you that we are commanded to love? How is it possible to make ourselves love someone?

TRANSFORMED

Our relationships have a profound influence on us, especially relationships with our friends. For better or worse, we inevitably start to talk, act, and think like the people around us. Jesus tells us to prioritize our relationship with God. The more we grow in that relationship, the more it will change us from the inside out. The results will flow out to all our other relationships. In other words, as God influences us, we will become a godly influence on others. Look at what Paul said in Romans 12:1-2.

How would you describe what it means to be a "living sacrifice"?

"Therefore, brothers and sisters, in view of the mercies of God, I urge you to present your bodies as a living sacrifice, holy and pleasing to God; this is your true worship. Do not be conformed to this age, but be transformed by the renewing of your mind, so that you may discern what is the good, pleasing, and perfect will of God."

Romans 12:1-2, CSB

What do you think it means to be "transformed by the renewing of your mind"?

What do you think it means to be "conformed to this age"?

A relationship with God is not just something you add to your life; it's something that radically transforms your life. When we love Him with all our soul, mind, and strength, we are laying our lives down as a sacrifice. It is an act of humility when we say to God, "You have my whole life." When we humble ourselves in this way, God begins to transform us from the inside out.

The deeper we grow in our relationship with God, the more clearly we will know the purposes He has for us—His will. As God transforms us and we begin to understand His will more clearly, He will guide us in loving our neighbors as well. By following the first commandment (love God), we are better able to obey the second (love people).

PRIORITIES

How do we know what our current priorities are? Make a list below of some of the things that get the most from you. For example, what are the things you spend most of your time doing (skip activities like school that you're required to do)? Be honest!

Time

Money

Thoughts

Speech

Our priorities reveal the things we really love. According to your lists, what are your biggest priorities? Where does God rank?

IN SUMMARY

- Your relationship with God is the most valuable thing in your life.
- The closer our relationship with God, the more He will transform our character.
- We must make our relationship with God our first priority.
- The more we love God, the better we will understand how to love others.

PREPARING FOR THE GROUP DISCUSSION

One thing that stood out to me today is:

One question I have based on today's study is:

CLOSING PRAYER

Thank You, God, for Your love. Please help me to love others around me in the same way that You first loved me and help me to be wise about the people I spend my time with. Help me to prioritize my relationship with You this week.

WHILE YOU WATCH

As you watch the video, use the space provided to take notes or write down any thoughts and questions you may have.

DISCUSSION

Based on what you learned in the video and your personal Bible study days throughout the week, spend time discussing the questions below.

This week, Mike and Daniel shared that one of the obstacles that confuses people about the relationship God wants for them is that there are so many different definitions of love presented to us in the world.

How would you define love?

What are some things that you say you "love" (see page 42).

What has influenced your view of love?

What do you consider the three most important aspects of any relationship?

Has it been easy or difficult for you to accept that God wants a relationship with you because He loves you? Why?

At the end of each day this week you wrote down one main takeaway and one question you had. Take turns sharing one of your takeaways or questions with the group.

GOING DEEPER

Read 1 John 4:16:

> *"So we have come to know and to believe the love that God has for us. God is love, and whoever abides in love abides in God, and God abides in him."*

God is the perfect standard of love. Every other definition of love should be measured against His character to see if it is genuine. This means that if we want to see what love is, we need to look at God. If we want to see how this love is perfectly lived out in a human life, we should look to the example of Jesus.

Why is it important to measure other versions of love against God's standard, rather than measuring God by the standard of our earthly versions of love?

If the Christian definition of love is based on the personal character of God, what are other definitions of love based on?

How are other definitions of love different from the Christian definition? How are they similar?

What is something you can learn about love by looking at the example of Jesus?

In what ways does a relationship with God affect all other relationships?

In 1 Corinthians 13:4-7, which is often read at weddings, Paul was actually referring to how all Christians should treat each other, not just romantic couples.

> *⁴ Love is patient and kind; love does not envy or boast; it is not arrogant ⁵ or rude. It does not insist on its own way; it is not irritable or resentful; ⁶ it does not rejoice at wrongdoing, but rejoices with the truth. ⁷ Love bears all things, believes all things, hopes all things, endures all things.*

How has God displayed these characteristics throughout the story told in the Bible?

Which of these characteristics of love is the most important to you? Why?

Which of these characteristics of love is the most difficult for you to give to others? Why?

Which one of the characteristics Paul listed is most lacking in the world today? Why?

What is one way you can live out this characteristic in the coming week?

PREVIEW VIDEO

Watch the short video introducing *Reality 3: God's Invitation*. Your personal study days this week will further unpack this reality.

PRAYER AND DISMISSAL

As a group, share any prayer requests and spend time in prayer. You may want to write these requests below as a reminder to pray for the people in your group throughout the week.

God's Invitation

"For my thoughts are not your thoughts, neither are your ways my ways," declares the Lord. "As the heavens are higher than the earth, so are my ways higher than your ways and my thoughts than your thoughts."

ISAIAH 55:8-9 (NIV)

"Follow me, and I will make you fishers of men." Immediately they left their nets and followed him.

MATTHEW 4:19-20

"For God is working in you, giving you the desire and the power to do what pleases him."

PHILIPPIANS 2:13 (NLT)

AN EARLY WAKE-UP CALL

Our friend Susan woke up at 4:45 in the morning with a strange feeling that she needed to pray for her neighbor Rhonda. Getting out of bed, she dropped to her knees and began to pray. A few minutes later, she felt God was telling her to call Rhonda. Although they were neighbors, they were not close friends. What would Rhonda think of being awakened so early? Susan reluctantly dialed the number and let it ring until Rhonda answered.

"Hello," Susan said nervously. "I'm so sorry to call you this early, but I felt God wanted me to tell you that He loves you." They exchanged some awkward small talk and then Susan invited Rhonda to a Bible study at her house and they hung up. Susan felt foolish. Had she just completely freaked her neighbor out?

When it came time for the Bible study, Rhonda was the first person to arrive and she was early. She then told Susan her side of the story. She had been awake much earlier than usual that morning. For weeks she had been wondering if God was real and if He loved her. Standing in the shower, she prayed for the first time in her life: "God, if you are real, would you forgive me of my sins?" As she stepped out of the shower, she heard her phone ringing. It was Susan, who had felt like God woke her up and led her at that very minute to tell Rhonda that God loved her and wanted a relationship with her. Rhonda began a relationship with Jesus that day and was later baptized on Easter Sunday.

Can you see the realities we've been looking at for the past two weeks play out in this story? God was at work all around Rhonda, and He was pursuing a love relationship with her. In the process, God also invited Susan to be a part of what He was doing.

Recognizing where God is at work is only part of the story; He also invites us to join Him in that work. This week, we're going to unpack *Reality 3: God invites you to become involved with Him in His work.*

Invited into Something More

"Follow me, and I will make you fishers of men." Immediately they left their nets and followed him.

Matthew 4:19-20

DAY 1

PART OF SOMETHING BIGGER

Have you ever wanted to be a part of something bigger than yourself? Chomping popcorn and binge-watching our way through a show on our favorite streaming service is fine for a weekend, but we soon get restless. This discontentment is what drives people to brave the sweaty crowds and overpriced food at conventions. Whatever our passion is—comics, music, video games, cats (why?)—we are not happy just to enjoy it in isolation; we want to feel a sense of community.

It's not just about being a part of something; we also desire to give ourselves to something. We want our lives to be more than just breathing air and eating food. This desire is why involvement in humanitarian and activist causes are increasing. We are realizing that living only for ourselves does not make us happy. As we will see today, the God of the universe invites you to join His exciting, sometimes terrifying global mission and purpose, which is far beyond anything you can imagine.

GOD'S INVITATION

The pages of the Bible are filled with stories of God calling people to join Him in His work. God does not tell people in the Bible like Moses, Paul, and Mary only what He has already done, but also what He plans to do through them. We see the same pattern in the life of Jesus:

> *18 As he was walking along the Sea of Galilee, he saw two brothers, Simon (who is called Peter), and his brother Andrew. They were casting a net into the sea—for they were fishermen. 19 "Follow me," he told them, "and I will make you fish for people." 20 Immediately they left their nets and followed him. 21 Going on from there, he saw two other brothers, James the son of Zebedee, and his brother John. They were in a boat with Zebedee their father, preparing their nets, and he called them. 22 Immediately they left the boat and their father and followed him.*

Matthew 4:18-22 (CSB)

Why do you think Jesus invited others to join Him instead of doing it by Himself?

Why do you think Jesus invited fishermen, instead of people who were richer, more powerful, or influential?

What do you think Jesus meant by the phrase, "I will make you fish for people"?

There is nothing wrong with being a fisherman. But Jesus invited these guys to join something bigger than the dreams they had for their own lives. They got to see the dead brought back to life, demons cast out, and the start of a global movement. Not bad for a group of small-town fishermen. In fact, even their fishing became miraculous when they got around Jesus (Luke 5:1-11).

We may read the Bible and think, "Well, that was nice for those guys, but will Jesus ever invite me to follow Him like that?" Jesus said, "If anyone would come after me, let him deny himself and take up his cross and follow me" (Matt. 16:24). He is already extending a call to us. If we want to become a disciple of Jesus, we must accept His invitation to follow Him.

FOLLOW THE LEADER

We sometimes feel like we need to do things for God rather than with God. As a result, we can end up doing the wrong things even though we may have the right intentions. Through the prophet Isaiah, God said, "My thoughts are not your thoughts, neither are your ways my ways. . . . For as the heavens are higher than the earth, so are my ways higher than your ways and my thoughts than your thoughts" (Isa. 55:8-9). If we want to be involved in God's activity, He must show us how because we do not instinctively know what to do. As you follow His lead, you will experience more than you ever could have through your own efforts.

GOD AT WORK ON A COLLEGE CAMPUS

When our grandfather was a pastor, a lot of college students attended his church. They desired to see Bible studies start in the dorm rooms of the local university. But no matter how hard they tried, they couldn't get anything going. One Sunday, our grandpa challenged them to follow God's lead. He said, "This week, don't try to do something for God. Instead, pray. Then look to see where God is at work and join Him."

Three days later, one of the young ladies was sitting in class when a fellow student approached her. The student asked, "Are you a

In the 1992 animated film, *Aladdin*, Princess Jasmine gets to experience the thrill of soaring through the skies on a magic carpet. It required stepping out in faith when Aladdin asked her, "Do you trust me?"[1] Similarly, if we want to experience all that Jesus has for us, it will involve stepping out in trust to follow Him into the unknown.

Christian? Because several other girls in our dorms have been wanting to study the Bible, but none of us have read it before and we need someone to help us understand what we are reading." God was clearly inviting the young lady from the church into His activity. Throughout the next few months, they started several Bible studies in both the men and women's dorms, which resulted in many students coming to know Jesus. We're glad because all this activity on campus led to a thriving young adults group at the church. And guess who eventually became a Christian as a result of that church at the university? Our mom, when she was eighteen years old.

What sort of things might prevent us from seeing God's activity around us?

What advantage is there to following God's lead rather than simply asking Him to follow us?

Why is it difficult to trust that God's plans for us are better than what we dream for ourselves?

Those fishermen had no idea all that they were about to experience when they stepped out of their boats to follow Jesus. There are adventures waiting for you too.

Are you ready to follow God's lead and join in His activity?

IN SUMMARY

- The Bible is filled with stories of God inviting people to join in His work.
- God wants to include us in what He is doing too.
- God's plans won't always match our plans.
- If we want to experience God's best, we must follow Him, not ask Him to follow us.

PREPARING FOR THE GROUP DISCUSSION

One thing that stood out to me today is:

One question I have based on today's study is:

CLOSING PRAYER

Thank You, God, that You choose to involve people in Your activity. Please show me what You are doing around me this week and help me know how You want me to join You.

No Ordinary People

"For God is working in you, giving you the desire and the power to do what pleases him."

PHILIPPIANS 2:13 (NLT)

DAY 2

"GOD COULD NEVER USE ME"

"What am I doing here?" Have you ever asked yourself that question? Perhaps you were about to step onto the field for a big sporting event, take the stage for an important recital, or sit down to take a difficult test. Did you feel inadequate, like you didn't have what it took to complete the challenge in front of you? When you hear us talking about joining God in what He is doing, does it make you nervous that you'll end up in a situation you're not ready for? We'll be honest: it makes us nervous too!

What are three things you're nervous God might ask you to do?

Why did you pick these three things?

We're both guilty of saying, "God could never use me!" This statement doesn't just reveal what we believe about ourselves (that we are inadequate); it also reveals what we believe about God (that He is inadequate, too). The apostle Paul described God as being "able to do far more abundantly than all that we ask or think, according to the power at work within us" (Eph. 3:20).

GOD USES UNLIKELY PEOPLE

In the Bible, God always seemed to choose unlikely people to join Him in His work. Moses is a good example. When God first called him, the people of Israel were slaves in Egypt. Moses was a fellow Hebrew who had been adopted into the household of Pharaoh (Egypt's king), but he ended up committing murder and fleeing to the desert as a fugitive. Years later, God spoke to him from a burning bush and commanded him to go back to Egypt with a message for Pharaoh: "Let my people go!" Take a look at how Moses responded to God:

"Who am I that I should go to Pharaoh and bring the children of Israel out of Egypt?" (Ex. 3:11).

"If I come to the people of Israel and say to them, 'The God of your fathers has sent me to you,' and they ask me, 'What is his name?' what shall I say to them?" (Ex. 3:13).

"But behold, they will not believe me or listen to my voice, for they will say, 'The Lord did not appear to you'" (Ex. 4:1).

"Oh, my Lord, I am not eloquent, either in the past or since you have spoken to your servant, but I am slow of speech and of tongue" (Ex. 4:10).

"Oh, my Lord, please send someone else" (Ex. 4:13).

In these verses, what were some of the excuses Moses used to try to avoid God's call?

Which of these excuses can you most relate to? Why?

Moses felt completely inadequate, but that's not the end of the story. God ultimately used Moses to become one of the greatest men of faith history has ever seen! Moses may have only seen inevitable failure in his future, but God had bigger plans. What can God do through you?

GOD USES YOUNG PEOPLE

As a teenager, have you ever been told that you are a future leader? Sometimes in today's culture, even in churches, there is a mindset that the teen years are just a training period to prepare us to join God's activity once we're older. This mentality can understandably lead to a belief that only adults are ready for a vibrant relationship with God. In fact, there is evidence that those who stick with their faith long-term as adults are the ones who were invited as teens to join the adults in worship.[2]

The Bible provides many examples of God working through young people. Some of the greatest biblical heroes were young. Think of Josiah (2 Kings 22:1-23,30), Joseph (Gen. 37–50), David (1 Sam. 16:1–17:58), Esther (Esther 1–10), Daniel and his friends (Dan. 1:17), Mary (Luke 1:26-56), Jeremiah (Jer. 1:4-12), and Timothy (2 Tim. 1:3-7). Don't count yourself out just because you are young. God can use you to set an example for older generations (1 Tim. 4:12).

Much about the younger generation today sets you up to be used mightily by God. You are part of the largest and most ethnically diverse generation in history.[3] What could God do through your generation if you choose to follow Him?

IDA SCUDDER

Ida Scudder's grandfather was the first medical missionary to go from the United States to India. His ten children followed in his footsteps! Ida respected her parents' decision, but she wanted something else for her life. She thought she was just not the type to become a missionary. Then her mom got sick, so Ida traveled to India to care for her.

One night, a local man knocked on their door. His young wife was having a baby, but she was experiencing severe complications. Ida's father, a doctor, offered to go help, but the man (a priest of the local religion) refused. According to his beliefs, another man could not see his wife in those circumstances. Two more men came to them with the same problem. Without Ida's mother and with Ida having no medical training, there were no women who could help. Ida was devastated when all three young mothers died in childbirth. Then God gave her an invitation: "Move here and join Me in the work I am doing." Despite her fears of being inadequate for the giant task God was calling her to, she obeyed.

Ida returned to the States and spent the next several years training to become a doctor. She then moved to India and devoted the remainder of her life to caring for the people there. During her funeral procession, the road was lined for miles with the individuals she had helped, an honor normally only seen for royalty. Ida had plans for her life, but God had a much bigger story He wanted her to join.

WHAT ABOUT YOU?

You may not feel smart enough, talented enough, popular enough, attractive enough, or confident enough for God to use you. Guess what? You're exactly the type of person God delights in using! You might not feel capable, but God is. Don't set limits on what God can do through anyone's life— including yours. Philippians 2:13 says, " For God is working in you, giving you the desire and the power to do what pleases him." God will equip you for everything He invites you to do.

Do you believe that God sees more in you than you are able to see in yourself?

"God called me, and God knows where best a life should be spent."[1]

—Ida Scudder

IN SUMMARY

- God has often used the most unlikely people to accomplish His purposes.
- Don't count yourself out just because you are young.
- Don't let any excuse stand in the way of your obedience to what God is leading you to do.
- The same God who invites you will also equip you for His work.

PREPARING FOR THE GROUP DISCUSSION

One thing that stood out to me today is:

One question I have based on today's study is:

CLOSING PRAYER

Thank You, God, for inviting me into Your activity. Please give me the courage to follow You wherever You lead. Use my life to do great things this week I never thought possible.

God-Centered or Me-Centered?

"For my thoughts are not your thoughts, neither are your ways my ways," *declares the* LORD. *"As the heavens are higher than the earth, so are my* *ways higher than your ways and my thoughts than your thoughts."*

ISAIAH 55:8-9 (NIV)

DAY 3

BUSY PLANNING

Four aspiring comic book writers gathered at Midtown Comics in New York City to review their portfolios. They offered each other critiques and ideas for improvement in hopes of one day achieving their dream of becoming professional comic book writers. Someone outside their group took an interest in their work and asked if he could have a closer look. The four men told him not to bother them and they resumed their passionate discussion. The man walked away and they never realized that the stranger was, in fact, C. B. Cebulski—the influential talent scout and eventual editor-in-chief for Marvel Comics![5]

Those four writers could have been on the verge of joining something beyond their wildest dreams, but they were distracted by their own plans and ideas. We can sometimes treat God the same way. There is a bumper sticker that says, "Jesus is my copilot." But God is not our sidekick. Rather, we are invited to go along with Him for the journey He wants to take us on.

LISTEN TO HIM

Picture this scene: Three of the twelve disciples, Peter, James, and John, went with Jesus up a mountain to pray. Suddenly, Jesus began to glow pure white. The disciples had observed some astonishing miracles already, but this one took things to a whole new level. Then Elijah and Moses—two famous and long-gone heroes—joined the party and appeared standing with Jesus! In the middle of this amazing encounter, Peter decided to speak up: "Master, it is good that we are here. Let us make three tents, one for you and one for Moses and one for Elijah" (Luke 9:33).

Peter was thinking out loud, but he didn't get very far. "As he was saying these things, a cloud came and overshadowed them, and they were afraid as they entered the cloud. And a voice came out of the cloud, saying, 'This is my Son, my Chosen One; listen to him!'" (Luke 9:34-35).

God spoke down from heaven to tell Peter to stop talking. Talk about embarrassing!

What was wrong with Peter's plan?

What do you think Peter's intentions were?

Peter's heart was probably in the right place. The problem was that God had far bigger plans than his. In one of the most astonishing moments in history, God was revealing the glory of Jesus, but Peter wanted to start giving Jesus suggestions for what they should do. Your very best plans of what you can do for God are far inferior to God's plans to work through you.

FROM ME OR FROM GOD?

How do we know if the ideas in our head are from us or God? I (Mike) remember a young man who visited our church. Our students met in a cafe with a stage, speakers, and lights. He informed me that he was a rapper and that we should be using the cafe venue to host open mic nights. He also suggested that I let him come on our summer trip so he could lead everyone in doing evangelism on the beach. I had only known him for five minutes! While it may have seemed like he was interested in doing all of these things for God, I had my doubts.

What in the above encounter might lead you to doubt that the visitor was following God's lead?

When I suggested that the guest start by getting involved in a smaller way, like helping clean up at the end of the night, he shrugged it off and never came back. He seemed to be interested in serving God only if he was in the spotlight. One way to determine if we're following God's lead is to compare our actions with what the Bible teaches. Jesus told a story about someone going to a party and choosing the most honored seat at a table:

> [10] "But when you are invited, go and sit in the lowest place, so that when your host comes he may say to you, 'Friend, move up higher.' Then you will be honored in the presence of all who sit at table with you. [11] For everyone who exalts himself will be humbled, and he who humbles himself will be exalted."
>
> Luke 14:10-11

If we're seeking to be in the spotlight, we are likely following our own lead, not God's.

Something else we know about ourselves is that we all want to be comfortable. So, if we are feeling led to do something that is uncomfortable and it lines up with what we read in Scripture, there is a good chance God may indeed be leading us in that direction.

What are some other ways we might discern whether our ideas are from us or God?

There were only a few witnesses to Peter's outburst, for which he was probably grateful! But today's technology has given us a platform unheard of in previous generations. Teens spend an average of almost three hours per day on social media.[6] It requires wisdom not to post things in the moment for everyone to see that we will one day regret.

GOD-CENTERED PRAYERS

Another way to know whether we are pursuing God's plans or our own ideas is by the way we pray.

What are the last three things you remember praying for?

1._____

2._____

3._____

Take a look at your list. Do you see any themes or patterns? Write some of your observations here:

Our grandpa used to say that he could determine what people's view of God was by listening to them pray. As you can imagine, there were not a lot of volunteers to pray before the meal at family gatherings.

When we pray, we sometimes wing it. We say whatever comes to mind, and since we are naturally self-centered, what comes out is usually about us. "Help me do my best at basketball tryouts." "Help me start feeling better." "Help me pass my biology exam." "Help me to get that summer job." "Help that girl in my class to notice me."

We typically come up with a goal or plan and then ask God to make it successful. Like Peter, we come into the awesome presence of God and then do all the talking. Listen to what Jesus said about prayer:

> *"Pray then like this: 'Our Father in heaven, hallowed be your name. Your kingdom come, your will be done, on earth as it is in heaven.'"*
>
> **Matthew 6:9-10**

Instead of offering God a list of your best ideas for what He should do, ask Him to help you see what He is already doing and where He wants you to join Him. God cares about the things you care about, but He also desires for you to experience much more than that.

ACTIVITY: WRITING OUT A PRAYER

In the space below or on blank piece of paper, write out a prayer. Follow the format provided but make it personal.

Dear God,

Thank God for His goodness.

Ask Him to reveal what He is doing around you.

Thank God for all that He is doing in your life.

Ask God for guidance and power to follow Him.

Are you ready for God to answer your prayer?

IN SUMMARY

- When we pray, we may need to listen more and talk less.
- God has bigger and better plans for your life than you can imagine.
- Our prayers reveal a lot about how we view God.
- In order to know God's will, we need to hear from Him.

PREPARING FOR THE GROUP DISCUSSION

One thing that stood out to me today is:

One question I have based on today's study is:

CLOSING PRAYER

Thank You, God, that You want more for my life than I want for myself. Please speak to me today. (Take two minutes of silence and listen.)

Recognizing God at Work

"Jesus answered them, 'My Father is working until now, and I am working....the Son can do nothing of his own accord, but only what he sees the Father doing. For whatever the Father does, the Son does likewise. For the Father loves the Son and shows him all that he himself is doing. And greater works than these will he show him, so that you may marvel.'"

John 5:17,19b-20

ON MY DAY OFF

When I (Daniel) was a teen, I spent several months in Athens, Greece, working with refugees. On a rare day off, I treated myself to a day cruise. I befriended a teenage girl traveling with her mother, and as the youngest passengers, we decided to stick together. We spent the day touring and even won a traditional Greek dance competition. She was intrigued to learn I was a Christian and peppered me with questions about the refugee work I was doing. At the end of the day, as we were bused back to the parking lot, she said, "This was a fun day, although I didn't enjoy all the old churches because I'm an atheist." She then added, "But you're cool, not like the other Christians I know." Looking back, I realized that while I thought I was taking a day off from serving God in Greece, God was inviting me to join His work in that girl's life, and I didn't even realize it!

When God pursues a love relationship with you, He is also inviting you to join Him in His mission. God is at work in the world all around you, and He wants you to join Him. How do we recognize where He is working? Today we'll look at three ways that may help.

RECOGNIZING GOD'S ACTIVITY

One of the most frustrating experiences in life is having the desire and passion to move forward but not knowing what the next step is.

Do you like to have a plan, or would you rather figure things out as you go? How might this preference affect your relationship with God?

Have you ever felt unsure about what God wanted you to do? When have you experienced this feeling?

We can sometimes think of God as the classic Batman villain, the Riddler. He leaves encoded messages for us to solve, leading us on a frantic chase to find Him. Is that what God is really like?

If God initiates a relationship with you and invites you to join His work, then He is not going to hide this opportunity from you. The problem is that we don't always recognize His activity. Here are a few helpful guidelines…

1. Start with the Relationship

Let's look at John 5:20:

"For the Father loves the Son…"

God's invitation to join Him comes out of a relationship with Him. We've heard people express their frustration at God for withholding His will, but they had ignored their Bible for weeks, rushed through their prayers, and were too busy to attend church. Jesus carved out specific time to spend alone with His father, even if it meant climbing a mountain (Mark 6:46, Luke 6:12, John 6:15).

Look at what Jesus said in John 10:27: "My sheep hear my voice, and I know them, and they follow me." How do sheep come to know the voice of their shepherd? By spending a lot of time together. If you want to recognize God's voice, you need to spend time with Him.

2. Pray and Watch to See What God Does Next

"…and shows him all that he himself is doing."

On one particularly crazy day when we were younger, our mother was driving us to and from various events. For lunch, she whipped into a McDonald's drive-thru, quickly ordered, and then peeled out again. We were on the other side of town before we realized that we'd forgotten to pick up our order at the next window!

Sometimes when our lives become full of activities, we pray for God to reveal His will to us and then rush off to our next thing. When you ask God to show you His will, make sure to watch for an answer. Often the problem is not that God is silent but that we aren't watching or listening for His answer.

One idea is to keep a prayer journal. As you pray for various people and things, make notes about how you've seen God at work. It's fun to look back at how God answered our prayers, and seeing His responses encourages us to be intentional about watching for His activity.

While I (Mike) was praying at our church one Sunday, two individuals came clearly to my mind. Neither were Christians. I felt a burden to pray for them. At the end of the service, one of those young men asked for a ride home. I had the whole car ride to talk with him about faith. As soon as I dropped him off, my phone rang. It was the other guy I had prayed for. He felt he needed to call me to talk. I encountered a lot of people that night, but thankfully, my eyes were open to the two people I needed to talk to. We can sometimes miss the obvious simply because we're not watching for it. Or we might see the opportunity clearly, but we come up with excuses not to engage in it.

3. Look For What Only God Can Do

"For the Father loves the Son and shows him all that he himself is doing. And greater works than these will he show him, so that you may marvel" (John 5:20).

What are things you believe only God could do?

Sometimes God's activity is obvious. The Bible is full of spectacular miracles. We've shared some cool stories in this book of times when God was clearly at work. But even these instances can be easily missed if we are not looking for them. Many people in Jesus's day saw Him perform miraculous healings but still did not follow Him.

There are less dramatic signs to watch for as well. Jesus said, "No one can come to me unless the Father who sent me draws him" (John 6:44). Any time people are seeking or asking questions about Jesus, you can be sure that God is at work drawing them. If He wasn't at work, then they wouldn't be drawn to Him.

Here's another one: talking about the Holy Spirit, Jesus said, "When he comes, he will convict the world about sin, righteousness, and judgment" (John 16:8). It's not our job to convince someone that they need God or that they are a sinner; the Holy Spirit does that. If your friends start asking or talking about their sin and a need to be freed from it, it may be that the Holy Spirit is at work in their lives, and He is giving you an opportunity to share the good news of Jesus with them.

WHERE IS GOD AT WORK AROUND YOUR LIFE?

Based on everything you have learned this week and using the guidelines above, write down any areas that you sense God may be at work around you:

In my own life:

In my family:

In my church:

In my school:

Are you actively watching for God's activity in your life?

IN SUMMARY

- God wants to show you where He is at work.
- Sometimes God will reveal His work when and where we least expect it.
- God's invitation to join Him comes out of His relationship with you.
- When you ask God to reveal His activity to you, make sure you are watching for an answer from Him.

PREPARING FOR THE GROUP DISCUSSION

One thing that stood out to me today is:

One question I have based on today's study is:

CLOSING PRAYER

Thank You, God, for all You are doing in the world. Please open my eyes to see where You are at work around me so that I can join You this week.

WHILE YOU WATCH

As you watch the video, use the space provided to take notes or write down any thoughts and questions you have.

DISCUSSION

Based on what you learned in the video and in your personal Bible study days throughout the week, spend time discussing the questions below.

> Why do you think God chooses to involve us in His work, rather than doing it all Himself?

> What is the difference between doing something for God and doing something with God?

This week began with a story about Susan being awakened early in the morning with the feeling that God wanted her to call her neighbor.

> Have you ever had an experience where you knew God was clearly inviting you to join Him? Share this experience with the group.

> What fears, doubts, or concerns might keep you from being obedient when God invites you to join Him?

On page 64, you wrote down three things you'd be nervous God might ask you to do. Share some of your answers with the group.

Why are you nervous that God might ask you to do these things?

What would give you confidence to be obedient to what God is calling you to do?

At the end of each day this week you wrote down one main takeaway and one question you had. Take turns sharing one of your takeaways or questions with the group.

GOING DEEPER

Throughout the Bible, God invited many different kinds of people to join what He was doing: A teenage peasant girl (Mary), a former prince and convicted murderer (Moses), a young shepherd boy (David), a religious zealot (Paul), some blue-collar fisherman (Peter and Andrew), an immigrant (Ruth), a queen (Esther), a government worker (Levi), and the list could go on and on. In fact, perhaps the only thing they had in common was that they all accepted God's invitation to follow.

When we read the stories about these people in the Bible we might assume that they were a lot different than us. We often view them as Christian superheroes, super spiritual, bold, and with unshakable faith. But the truth is that they struggled with the same fears and insecurities we do. One example of this is with God's invitation to the prophet Jeremiah when he was a young man. Read Jeremiah 1:4-12 (CSB) and then discuss the questions below.

> *4 The word of the Lord came to me: 5 I chose you before I formed you in the womb; I set you apart before you were born. I appointed you a prophet to the nations. 6 But I protested, "Oh no, Lord God! Look, I don't know how to speak since I am only a youth." 7 Then the Lord said to me: Do not say, "I am only a youth," for you will go to everyone I send you to and speak whatever I tell you.*
>
> *8 Do not be afraid of anyone, for I will be with you to rescue you. This is the Lord's declaration. 9 Then the Lord reached out his hand, touched my mouth, and told me: I have now filled your mouth with my words. 10 See, I have appointed you today over nations and kingdoms to uproot and tear down, to destroy and demolish, to build and plant. 11 Then the word of the Lord came to me, asking, "What do you see, Jeremiah?" I replied, "I see a branch of an almond tree." 12 The Lord said to me, "You have seen correctly, for I watch over my word to accomplish it."*

What was Jeremiah worried about?

Why was Jeremiah anxious about these things?

Do you ever worry about the same things? Why?

What was God's answer to Jeremiah's doubt?

What do you think it means for God to "consecrate" something (v. 5)?

What does it mean for God to know us even before we are born?

How does this affect the way you see yourself?

How does it affect the way you see others?

Jeremiah was nervous because he was "only a youth" (v. 6). How do you feel your society and church view teens?

What obstacles must God help you to overcome in order to accomplish great things as a young person?

When you see the variety of people that God used in the Bible, what does that teach you about God and how He chooses to work in the world?

PREVIEW VIDEO

Watch the short video introducing *Reality 4: God Speaks*.

PRAYER AND DISMISSAL

As a group, share any prayer requests and spend time in prayer. You may want to write these requests below as a reminder to pray for the people in your group throughout the week.

God Speaks

"But the Helper, the Holy Spirit, whom the Father will send in my name, he will teach you all things and bring to your remembrance all that I have said to you."

JOHN 14:26

"Now we have received not the spirit of the world, but the Spirit who is from God, that we might understand the things freely given us by God."

1 CORINTHIANS 2:12

"Do you not know that your bodies are temples of the Holy Spirit, who is in you, whom you have received from God?"

1 CORINTHIANS 6:19 (NIV)

RED

When I (Mike) was a student, I had an unforgettable experience. As I read my Bible, it seemed like every page I turned to talked about loving the poor. I had read these verses before, but this time they really jumped out to me.

Over the next few weeks, it felt like every teaching I heard at church mentioned God's call for us to love the poor. I couldn't sleep at night. My mind was racing. Was I loving the poor in my community? I prayed for God to show me what to do. Then I got a crazy idea. What if I went downtown, looked to see where God was at work among the poor and joined Him?

That Saturday I drove downtown, parked, and began to walk and pray. The square that was usually full of homeless people was unusually empty that day. As I crossed the street, I bowed my head and prayed, "God, I believe You have led me downtown. Please show me where You are at work." I looked up and ran straight into a man pushing a grocery cart filled with his possessions. After crossing the street together, we introduced ourselves. His name was Red, and he acted as if he had been expecting me. Intrigued, I offered to buy his lunch.

We spent the afternoon together. I told him some of my story but mostly listened to his. We fed birds in the park, and I gave him a Bible. He asked for a ride to the local Walmart, so we somehow fit his cart into the trunk of my car with the help of a few bungee cords and drove off.

When we finally pulled into the Walmart parking lot, the sun had begun to drop along with the temperature. I gave him a scarf I had in my car. As we said our goodbyes, he pulled a necklace out from his shirt. It read "I believe in angels." Through tears, he pointed to me and said, "You are the one I prayed that God would send me."

God knew and loved Red, and He wanted to bring along someone to display that love to him. I wasn't special, but I was available. In the process, God also taught me a lot and helped me to realize how much more I could have been doing all along.

Before He returned to heaven, Jesus promised to send the Holy Spirit as a Helper to His disciples (John 14:15-17,26). The Holy Spirit is a gift given to every believer (Acts 2:38), indwelling our lives (1 Cor. 6:19), to help us understand and live out everything God has done for us (1 Cor. 2:10-16). In what ways did the Holy Spirit speak in the story above?

This week we are going to dive in to *Reality 4: God speaks by the Holy Spirit through the Bible, prayer, circumstances, and the church to reveal Himself, His purposes, and His ways.* As we unpack these truths this week, what might the Holy Spirit want to say to you?

Through the Bible

For the word of God is living and effective and sharper than any double-edged sword, penetrating as far as the separation of soul and spirit, joints and marrow. It is able to judge the thoughts and intentions of the heart.

Hebrews 4:12 (CSB)

DAY 1

WHAT'S IT WORTH TO YOU?

It's usually better to be told about the giant anacondas slinking through the water before being encouraged to jump into the river to cool off. This is just one of several eye-opening experiences I (Daniel) had while boating down the Amazon River as a teen. I had joined a mission team to offer medical and spiritual aid to the villages we passed. At one particular stop, a young girl ran straight toward me, hollering and waving her arms. She gave me a handful of various trinkets. These modest valuables represented her family's entire life savings. "She knows it's not much," explained the translator, "but she hopes it's enough to trade for a Bible."

I'll never forget the look in that girl's eyes. I probably had a dozen Bibles at home (many untouched). What was the difference between that young girl and me? I respected the Bible as a source of important truths and guidelines; she valued the Bible because it led her to encounter God.

IDENTIFYING YOUR READING HABITS

How often do you typically read your Bible each week? (Be honest!)

When you do, how much do you usually read (a few verses, a chapter, a full book, etc.) and what do you generally read (New Testament, Old Testament, Psalms, Gospels, etc.)?

What keeps you from reading your Bible more? Choose any of the following options:

Too busy	It's outdated	I forget
I rarely "get anything" out of it	I don't trust it	It's difficult to understand
I don't like reading	I disagree with it	Reading is difficult
It's boring	Poor time management	Other_____

MORE THAN A RELIGIOUS REQUIREMENT

For some of you, perhaps the reason you don't spend much time reading the Bible is because it feels like a religious requirement or school assignment. A Christian should not read the Bible out of duty but out of desire. God speaks to us when we read the Bible; and if the God of the universe has something to say, we should want to hear it! The Bible helps us know how to practically understand how to live godly lives.

> [16] *"All Scripture is God-breathed and is useful for teaching, rebuking, correcting and training in righteousness,* [17] *so that the servant of God may be thoroughly equipped for every good work."*
>
> **2 Timothy 3:16-17 (NIV)**

What do you think it means for Scripture to be "God-breathed"?

Interestingly, another time God "breathed" in the Bible was to give life to Adam in the garden of Eden. The Bible is not just an ancient religious text, it's alive and active (Heb. 4:12). It is not just about God, it is from Him. This is why Christians call the Bible "God's Word." Whenever you open your Bible, you are encountering the divine Author.

GOD'S WORD

What are your expectations when you open your Bible? What (if anything) do you hope to get out of it?

Have you ever been disappointed when your Bible reading didn't meet those expectations?

The Bible is the highest-selling book of all time, and second-place isn't even close.[1] In fact, the Bible is the best-selling book of the year, every single year.[2]

There are roughly 25,000 manuscripts of the New Testament that have been found in ancient languages, including around 5,700 in the original Greek.[3,4] This allows experts to compare them and do something called "textual criticism." The more copies we have, the more confident we can be in determining what the original manuscripts said.

Some of the Bible is descriptive, meaning it describes what people did. Other parts of the Bible are prescriptive, meaning it tells us what we should do. We are not supposed to copy everything we read in the Bible, such as Ezekiel eating a scroll! (See Ezekiel 3:1-3.) However, the Holy Spirit can use anything in the Bible to speak into our lives.

Interesting Facts about the Bible: 1) 66 books with 40 different authors. 2) Longest name is Maher-shalal-hash-baz (Isa. 8:1). 3) Longest verse is Esther 8:9 at 78 words. 4) Shortest verse is John 11:35, "Jesus wept." 5) Shortest book by number of words is 3 John. 6) Dogs are mentioned approximately 42 times and cats are never referenced. 7) There are 185 songs in the Bible. 8) The longest chapter is Psalm 119 with 176 verses. 9) The longest book is Psalms with 150 chapters. 10) The last word in the Bible is "Amen" (Rev. 22:21).

If we approach the Bible with misguided expectations, we can easily become frustrated and confused. Have you ever heard someone ask, "Does the Bible really say that Christians shouldn't _____?" This approach assumes the Bible is nothing more than a rulebook. Satan actually used this same way of thinking to tempt Adam and Eve, saying, "Did God actually say, 'You shall not eat of any tree in the garden?'" (Gen. 3:1). The primary purpose of the Bible isn't to make us "good people." Jesus got frustrated when the religious leaders of his day approached the Scriptures like this but missed Him (John 5:39).

The Bible is also not intended to be a "religious textbook," full of quick answers to every possible question. If it tried to answer all our questions, it would be approximately 875,384,496 pages longer than it already is! Instead of giving us a divinely inspired Wikipedia, God did something far more valuable through Scripture—He revealed Himself. The Bible is primarily about God—who He is, what He has done in history, and how He desires us to know Him.

In this way, the Bible is less like a detailed step-by-step walkthrough for a video game and more like immersing yourself in the game itself. That's why it is important to read your Bible regularly. The more time you spend in God's Word, the more you come to know His heart and character, recognize His voice, and understand the way He works in the world.

What might God want to say to you through His Word?

IN SUMMARY

- The Bible is not just about God, it is from God.
- The Bible was not intended as a religious textbook.
- Christians should read the Bible out of desire, not duty.
- When you read the Bible, the Holy Spirit is at work applying it to your life.

PREPARING FOR THE GROUP DISCUSSION

One thing that stood out to me today is:

One question I have based on today's study is:

CLOSING PRAYER

God, thank You for giving us Your Word. Holy Spirit, please help me to understand and apply the truths of Scripture to my life as I read it this week.

Through Prayer

"Call to Me and I will answer you and tell you great and incomprehensible things you do not know."

Jeremiah 33:3

IN THE NICK OF TIME

A few years ago, God led me (Mike) to move my family nearly three thousand miles away from our home in Atlanta, Georgia, to Victoria, Canada, to start a church. When we arrived, all we had were two suitcases and a temporary one-bedroom suite on top of a mountain. Since we didn't have a church building, we had a list of several specific things we believed we needed if our house was going to be the home base for our ministry. Victoria is an extremely difficult housing market, and despite searching desperately for several months, we couldn't find a long-term living space. Our moving company informed us that our truck of household goods was arriving on February 2nd, whether we had a place for it or not!

Discouraged, my wife Sarah prayed, "God, we believe you have called us here. We are running out of time. Please provide." Then she felt God saying, "Look one more time." Although she had just spent hours searching for houses, Sarah opened her laptop and refreshed the page. There was a new listing. In fact, it had just been posted during her prayer and was everything we had been praying for. Sarah quickly emailed the landlord, and out of a long list of interested people, they chose us. They said, "You were the first ones to contact us and there was something about your family. We felt like you were the ones who needed to be here." They told us we could move in on February first—the day before our moving truck arrived.

GOD SPEAKS THROUGH PRAYER

It's not uncommon to treat prayer as a monologue rather than a dialogue. Prayer is not just how we talk to God, it is also one of the most important ways that God communicates to us. When you pray, are you also listening?

Let's look at the example of Jesus. A lot of people wanted to be around Him. How was He able to narrow it down and choose His twelve closest disciples? Did He check their resumes? Did they have a talent competition? Did they take a test? Nope. Jesus prayed.

12 In these days he went out to the mountain to pray, and all night he continued in prayer to God. 13 And when day came, he called his disciples and chose from them twelve, whom he named apostles.

Luke 6:12-13

What are three observations that stand out to you when you read the verses above?

We know that God answered Jesus's prayer because of another prayer in John 17:6,9: "I have manifested your name to the people whom you gave me out of the world. Yours they were, and you gave them to me, and they have kept your word. . . . I am praying for them. I am not praying for the world but for those whom you have given me, for they are yours." The Father led Jesus to know which disciples to choose. This was a huge decision. Just three years later Jesus would send these men out to spread the gospel message around the world (Matt. 28:16-20).

Is it easy or difficult for you to pray? Why or why not?

Is it easier for you to listen or speak when you are in a conversation with someone else? Why?

Has God ever spoken to you while you were praying? If so, what was that like?

DISTRACTIONS AND PRIORITIES

How many times have you looked at your phone since getting started today? Be honest! We live in a time in history when it is very easy to be distracted and it's very hard to be quiet. There are hundreds of things that can pull our attention away from taking time to listen. Fifty-five percent of young people today use their smartphones more than five hours per day.[5] Today there are a lot of people trying to get your attention through your phones, tablets, or laptops. In fact, these digital distractions are run by algorithms that are specifically designed to know how best to get and keep your attention. But distractions are not necessarily new. There was a reason why Jesus often retreated to mountains to pray. Crowds of people were constantly trying to get His attention too, and He knew that spending time in prayer had to be a priority.

Having our minds distracted all the time has some serious side-effects. Psychologists have found that a calm and attentive mind is needed for important things like empathy and compassion.[4] Constantly shifting our attention takes more energy than focusing, so distractions wear us down mentally. In fact, the fast-paced stimulation of much media today negatively affects our brain's ability to focus, achieve goals, solve problems, remember things, have self-control, and be patient.[5]

List the top three things that might distract you from praying, being silent, or taking time to listen for God. Beside each, write one suggestion of how you might avoid or overcome that distraction.

Distraction

How to Avoid or Overcome
the Distraction

What are five things that you have made important priorities in your life? List anything that you are intentional to give time and attention to.

Is prayer on this list? Why or why not?

If you really want to hear from God, then prayer must become a priority not a pastime. Every healthy relationship is built on communication. Prayer is a way we communicate with God, and it can be how He communicates with us.

Are you willing to set aside time each day to spend time in prayer?

IN SUMMARY

- Every healthy relationship is built on communication.
- Prayer should be a two-way conversation where we speak and listen.
- There are many things that can distract you from praying.
- Prayer must be a priority not a pastime.

PREPARING FOR THE GROUP DISCUSSION

One thing that stood out to me today is:

One question I have based on today's study is:

CLOSING PRAYER

God, thank You for the ability You have given me to pray anytime and anywhere. Please help me to make prayer a priority in my life. Guard my heart and mind from distractions today.

Circumstances

"As for you, you meant evil against me, but God meant it for good, to bring it about that many people should be kept alive, as they are today."

Genesis 50:20

BEHIND DOOR NUMBER ONE

When I (Mike) was younger, I lived in a small apartment attached to my aunt and uncle's house. One weekend my friend Dave crashed at my place while I was out of town. He arrived extremely late, found the key, and tried the door. It didn't work. He noticed another door and tried the key there. It opened! He walked in and found the bedroom, but there was a problem: it was our aunt and uncle's part of the house, and they had no idea who this person was in their bedroom door in the middle of the night. Luckily, Dave was able to quickly explain before my uncle had a chance to call the cops.

OPEN DOORS

Dave discovered that an open door is not necessarily an invitation to enter. We can sometimes think that any open door in front of us—a college acceptance, a romantic relationship, a summer job opportunity, and so on—is God's will. This is a dangerous way to live. There is an interesting story in 2 Samuel 5:17-25. David was a man of war, but before rushing into battle with the Philistines, he checked with God on two different occasions. The first time he got the green light to enter into battle. The second time, God gave him some further instructions on how to go into battle. David certainly didn't want to rush into these open doors without assurance that God would go with him. Otherwise, he might end up like the Israelite army in Numbers 14:39-45 who went into battle despite God's warnings and were soundly defeated.

> Briefly describe a time when you did something you thought was a good idea, only to realize later that you shouldn't have done it.

> What made you think the above opportunity was the right thing to do?

Circle the options that best describe how you usually make decisions:

Do what "feels right"   Ask advice from friends and family

Make a "pros" and "cons" list   Pray about it

Do whatever is easiest   Do whatever makes me the most happy

Choose whatever outcome   Put it off until the opportunity
benefits me most   has passed

Try to get someone else to make   Other: _____
the decision for me

STRANGE CIRCUMSTANCES

Proverbs 3:5-6 tells us not to trust in our own understanding. Not every open door is the right path for us. Similarly, not every closed door is a sign that it is the wrong path. God may want us to wait at the door patiently and keep knocking until the time is right for Him to open it. This is why we need God's wisdom to properly understand our circumstances.

In Acts 16:6-10, Paul and his crew were traveling and preaching, but they were prevented from entering a certain city. Paul had a dream of a man saying, "Come over to Macedonia and help us" (v. 9). He concluded that God was calling them there, so that's where they went. Along the way they met a woman named Lydia who became a believer, along with her entire household. Later, they cast out a demon from a slave girl, and the authorities threw them in prison (Acts 16:16-24). It seems like another closed door. As it turns out, God had something else for them to do in the prison. An earthquake opened all the prison doors (talk about an open door opportunity), but instead of escaping like you would expect, Paul and Silas stayed and led the jailer and his whole family into a relationship with Jesus. The next day, the authorities decided to let them go anyway (Acts 16:25-40).

How many different closed and opened doors are there in the above story?

Describe a past circumstance in your life that seemed hopeless, but then turned around in a surprising way:

Describe a weird coincidence in your life that is difficult to explain:

MORE THAN A COINCIDENCE

The Bible is filled with examples of God doing miracles. These aren't always big "wow" moments. The truth is, whenever God chooses to act in a situation, it communicates something. (This is why the Gospel of John calls them "signs.") Sometimes, timing can help us see more clearly God's activity.

When I (Mike) moved to Victoria to plant a church, we did not have a worship leader. Soon after moving, I received an opportunity to speak at a youth conference near Calgary, Canada. I prayed: "Lord, you know our needs. Please use this opportunity to guide us to a worship pastor." At the conference, I was impressed with the young man leading the music and felt compelled to invite him to Victoria. He lived twenty hours away, and we had no money to pay him. But guess what? His current job was just about to end, and he had been praying that God would help him know what to do next.

Several weeks later I received another opportunity to speak, this time in Hilton Head, South Carolina. Again, I prayed: "God, you know our needs, and you know that we don't have the money to pay our worship leader. We need $20,000." In one of my talks at the conference, I shared how we were trusting God to provide everything we needed for planting the church. During the break, a woman handed me a check for $20,000! I later found out that she had just received that money and had been praying about where God wanted her to use it. In all these situations, God was responding to the prayers of His people and seemed to be lining up our circumstances to keep us all moving on the right path.

EYES OPEN

We are not saying "everything happens for a reason." It can be dangerous to see every circumstance as more than a coincidence. Even so, God can use your circumstances to give you clarity about what He wants you to do. He will also confirm these things through prayer, the Bible, and other people. When these things all line up, God may be leading you forward.

Do you recognize God in your circumstances?

IN SUMMARY

- Not every open door in our lives is God's will for us.
- Watch to see what God does after you pray.
- The timing of our circumstances can help us see God at work.
- God will confirm your circumstances through the Bible, prayer, and other people.

PREPARING FOR THE GROUP DISCUSSION

One thing that stood out to me today is:

One question I have based on today's study is:

CLOSING PRAYER

Thank You, God, for Your activity in and around my life. Please open my eyes to understand my circumstances this week.

Through the Church

"So in Christ we, though many, form one body, and each member belongs to all the others."

Romans 12:5 (NIV)

ORGANIZED RELIGION

You may have heard the famous quote, often attributed to Gandhi, "I like your Christ, I do not like your Christians. Your Christians are so unlike your Christ."[6] One recent survey revealed that roughly ten percent of all Americans fell into the category: "Love Jesus but not the church."[7] The hashtag #ImAChristianBut makes the social media rounds every few months as Christians seek to distance themselves from the broader Christian religion. For younger generations, it is often not Jesus they have a problem with but their poor experience with church that has pushed them away.[8] Has this been your experience?

What comes to mind when you hear the term "organized religion"?

If you had to describe the church in five words, what would they be?

1. _____   2. _____   3. _____

4. _____   5. _____

Have you ever been embarrassed to be associated with the Christian church? If so, why did you feel this way?

Is church involvement important for a Christian? Why or why not?

After over 2000 years, the Christian church brings a lot of baggage with it. Perhaps you, like many others, have wondered, "What's the point? If Christianity is a relationship with God, then why bother with all the hypocrites in the church?" The answer to that question is simply this—because the church is God's plan, and it is also one of the ways that He will speak to you.

AN IMPERFECT FAMILY

Sarah was just four years old when she tragically lost her father in a snowmobile accident. When she was sixteen, a school friend invited her to church. She was not religious, but agreed to go. That Sunday happened to be Father's Day. The pastor preached on Psalm 68:5-6 (CSB), "God in his holy dwelling is a father of the fatherless and a champion of widows. God provides homes for those who are deserted." Shortly after, Sarah became a Christian and went on her first mission trip to Africa to minister to orphans and share the sense of belonging she had found. (And four years later, she became Daniel's wife.)

One of the best metaphors for the church is a family. Whatever your earthly family is like, the Bible says that when you become a Christian you are adopted into the family of God: "He predestined us to be adopted as sons through Jesus Christ for himself, according to the good pleasure of his will" (Eph. 1:5, CSB).

Like all families, the church is not perfect. As brothers, we remember the last physical fight we ever had. We were teens and a playful taunt about a fantasy hockey team led to a rumble that ended with a giant hole in the wall. A strategically-placed shelf hid the hole for years until our family sold the house and our father finally discovered it. Thankfully, the hole was just in the wall and not in our relationship. For others, the damage is more personal. We've had friends abused—emotionally and sexually—in the church. Not long after joining, Sarah (from the story above) had petty church members mail her a forged letter from the "church leadership" informing her that she had been kicked out for being such an awful sinner.

Have you ever been let down or hurt by your church family? In what ways?

How did this make you feel about God's people?

The Bible says in 1 Corinthians 12:26, "If one member suffers, all suffer together; if one member is honored, all rejoice together." In other words, being a part of God's family is a roller coaster ride, but family remains family through the highs and lows. Our pastor once had an angry Christian declare, "The church is full of hypocrites," to which he responded, "It is, and there's always room for one more!"

The apostle Paul had to address some pretty messed-up stuff going on in the church at times (see 1 Cor. 5:1), but he never said, "This church thing just isn't working out, let's come up with another plan!" It's good news that there is room in the church for imperfect people, because that's all of us! Jesus Himself called the church "His" and promised to be its chief builder (Matt. 16:18). When the church acts in sin, it is because we've attempted to take over these responsibilities from Jesus, rather than follow His plan.

GOD SPEAKS THROUGH PEOPLE

The potential for hurt makes it tempting to go with a "just me and God" attitude. However, as our uncle often says, "Our relationship with God is extremely personal, but it was never meant to be private." One of the ways God will speak to you is through other members of the family. Do you remember the testimony Daniel shared in the first week about his insomnia? (See page 15.) God used a member of the church family to write a letter and share His love when Daniel needed it most, and then used Daniel to do the same to others in need.

I (Mike) remember kneeling at the front of our church and praying that God would clearly let us know if He wanted us to move to Canada. Immediately afterwards, a man (who had no idea that we were even considering a move) came up to me and said, "God is about to call you to somewhere else, and your answer is 'Yes, Lord.'" This happened several other times over the next few weeks as God used members of the church to confirm His calling on our lives.

Has God ever used another Christian to give you guidance or encouragement just when you needed it? If so, describe the experience below.

Has God ever used you to give someone else guidance or encouragement just when they needed it? If so, describe the experience below.

This should not come as a surprise as we read through Scripture and see how the Holy Spirit works. In Acts 9:10-19, God used a man named Ananias to heal, baptize, and confirm Saul (eventually known as Paul) as a missionary. Paul later taught that the Holy Spirit gives various gifts to people in the church like wisdom, knowledge, healing, miracles, prophecy, and so on (1 Cor. 12:1-11). These gifts are not given for selfish use; they are given to help others in the church. This is why Paul used the metaphor of a body when speaking about the church (1 Cor. 12:12-31). If parts of the body aren't communicating with each other, things are not going to go well. How can we expect to be in the middle of God's will if we separate ourselves from the rest of the body? How can we benefit from the gifts of the Spirit when we have removed ourselves from our Christian brothers and sisters?

Paul used the metaphor of different parts of one body to describe the family of God. Based on everything you've read in this week, what is another visual for how God desires the church to function?

In the space below, write out your metaphor or visualize it with a drawing.

God wants to use your church family to speak into your life, and He wants to use you to speak into theirs. Are you ready and willing to be an active member in the family of God through the local church?

IN SUMMARY

- Many young people are okay with Jesus, but not okay with the church.
- When you become a Christian, other Christians become your spiritual family.
- Like all families, the church is filled with imperfect people.
- The Holy Spirit empowers people in the church to build each other up.

PREPARING FOR THE GROUP DISCUSSION

One thing that stood out to me today is:

One question I have based on today's study is:

CLOSING PRAYER

God, thank You for adopting me into Your family. I know I can be hypocritical just like everyone else, so please give me the patience to see and love my church family the way that You see and love me.

WHILE YOU WATCH

As you watch the video, use the space provided to take notes or write down any thoughts and questions you have.

DISCUSSION

Based on what you learned in the video and your personal Bible study days throughout the week, spend time discussing the questions below.

In the video and in your personal study days this week, you learned about four ways that God speaks to people—Bible, prayer, experiences, and the church.

Why do you think God chooses to speak to us in different ways, rather than using the same method each time?

Which one of these ways have you experienced the most in your own life?

Which of these four ways is most difficult for you? Why?

Can you share an example with the group of a time when God clearly spoke to you through one of these four methods?

Have you ever been unsure whether it was God speaking to you or just your own desires leading you? How did you seek clarity? How do we know the difference?

This week began with Mike telling the story of meeting a homeless man named Red.

What stood out most to you in that story?

At the end of each day this week you wrote down one main takeaway and one question you had. Take turns sharing one of your takeaways or questions with the group.

GOING DEEPER

One of the most important truths in Scripture is not necessarily how God speaks but that He speaks. At the same time, we need to be careful. Claiming, "God told me…" can easily be abused to try and justify things we want to do, rather than things God is leading us to do. For example, it can be manipulative for someone to insist their romantic crush go out with them because, "God told me we are supposed to be together." How does the other person know that God said this?

This is why it's important to have the "checks and balances" of these four different ways God speaks. If what you think God is telling you in your prayers or through your circumstances is clearly contradicted by what you read in the Bible, then it must not be from God, because God will not contradict Himself (Num. 23:19; Malachi 3:6; 2 Tim. 2:13; Heb. 13:8; James 1:17).

As a group, choose one or more of the following sections to study deeper together. If you are a larger group, then you can split up into four smaller teams and each take one, then come back and share together as a whole.

The Bible

Josiah became king when he was only 8 years old! Several years later, the "Book of the Law" (which most likely included the book of Deuteronomy) was discovered, after having been lost. Read 2 Kings 22:8–23:3 to see Josiah's response.

1. What was Josiah's response when these Scriptures were found?

2. What did God say to Josiah and his people?

3. What actions did Josiah take after hearing from God?

4. What are some examples from your own life of how God has used the Bible to speak to you?

5. How does our culture view the Bible today? Why?

Prayer

In the book of Acts we read about the disciples spreading the exciting news of Jesus to people who had not yet heard. There were some, like Cornelius, who were Gentiles. They believed in God, but did not yet understand who Jesus was. They needed further instruction. Read Acts 10:1-8,30-33 to see how God answered the prayers of Cornelius.

1. What do you notice about how God spoke through prayer? What was Cornelius's response?

2. How often did Cornelius pray? What are some distractions in our lives that keep us from praying more often?

3. Do you like to pray? Why or why not?

4. Cornelius was praying at the ninth hour, which was about 3:00 p.m. When is the easiest time of day for you to pray? Why?

5. What are some examples from your own life of how God has spoken to you through prayer?

Circumstances

Paul and Silas were traveling together and preaching the good news of Jesus. They faced constant opposition, but when their circumstances seemed hopeless, God would often lead them to just the right people at just the right time. Read Acts 16:6-40 and consider how God directed their circumstances.

1. What do you notice about how God worked through the various circumstances of Paul and Silas?

2. At what points could they have grown discouraged? Why didn't they?

3. How can we know that God is speaking to us in our circumstances, and that we are not just seeing what we want to see?

4. Do you believe in "coincidences"? Why or why not? How can you tell the difference?

5. What are some examples of how God has spoken to you through your circumstances?

The Church

Peter was the unofficial leader of the disciples and was known for being a very bold man. You can imagine how intimidating he might be. However, Paul was not intimidated when he saw Peter acting wrongly. Read Galatians 2:11-14 and note how God used Paul to speak truth into Peter's life.

1. What do you notice about how God used Paul to speak truth to Peter?

2. Why might it have been difficult for Paul to confront Peter?

3. Why is it important to have people in our lives who are not afraid to tell us hard things? What are the dangers of people only telling us what we want to hear?

4. Why is it sometimes difficult for us to take advice from other people, even if God is speaking through them?

5. What are some examples of how God has used other people in your life to speak to you?

PREVIEW VIDEO

Watch the video introducing *Reality 5: A Leap of Faith*.

PRAYER AND DISMISSAL

As a group, share any prayer requests and spend time in prayer. You may want to write these requests below as a reminder to pray for the people in your group throughout the week.

A Leap of Faith

*"He did this so that all the peoples of the earth might know that the hand of the L*ORD* is powerful and so that you might always fear the L*ORD* your God."*

JOSHUA 4:24 (NIV)

"Why do you call me 'Lord, Lord,' and not do what I tell you?"

LUKE 6:46

For we walk by faith, not by sight.

2 CORINTHIANS 5:7

Humble yourselves, therefore, under the mighty hand of God so that at the proper time he may exalt you, casting all your anxieties on him, because he cares for you.

1 PETER 5:6-7

FROM THE CHAPEL TO THE ER

The summer I (Mike) graduated from high school, I faced a daunting question: what now? I didn't know what I wanted to do, but I knew what I didn't want to do—become a pastor. The thought of public speaking terrified me.

The end of summer quickly approached and I still had no post-graduation plan, so I signed up at the last minute for a year at the local Bible college where my father worked. If nothing else, it would buy me one more year to figure things out.

During the first month, the school held a "Spiritual Emphasis Week," featuring daily chapel services at noon. Being a responsible, dedicated student and knowing that my father was the president of the school, I skipped the first three chapel services. To be honest, I had not been feeling well. I attributed it to how busy I was as a full-time student and working a part-time job. But on Thursday, something changed.

I was on my way out again when I felt the urge to stop. I sensed God saying, "You need to stay for this one." I stood awkwardly in the doorway, my car in sight just a few feet away in the parking lot. Reluctantly, I turned around and found a seat at the back just in time to hear the speaker for the day.

He spoke about the Israelites in Exodus 14 running from the Egyptians and ending up at the Red Sea. When all seemed lost, God told them to "move forward." Then the speaker said, "God never takes us around our fears; He takes us through them." I realized then that God had been clearly calling me to become a pastor, but I was allowing my fear to hold me back. That morning I committed my future into God's hands. "Lord," I prayed, "Even though it scares me to death, if you are calling me to be a pastor, then I'll follow you in obedience."

Less than twenty-four hours later, I was laying in a hospital bed in the ER. I finally had an answer to why I had been feeling bad. I was a newly diagnosed Type-1 Diabetic. As I lay on the hospital bed in the middle of the night with nothing but the beeping of machinery and the glowing lights of medical equipment around me, God spoke to my heart again: "Mike, this has never been only about you being a pastor. It is about trusting Me with all your fears. If you trust Me, then I will take you through any fears you face, whether it is your calling as a pastor or your battle with diabetes. Whatever 'Red Sea' lies before you, I will take you through it."

Faith can be scary, but on the other side of your fears are the most amazing experiences you will ever have with God. Are you ready to face your fears, trust God, and take a leap of faith? This week we will unpack *Reality 5: God's invitation leads to a leap of faith that requires obedience.*

An Encounter with God Requires Faith

"For we walk by faith, not by sight."

2 Corinthians 5:7

DAY 1

PINK ELEPHANTS

If we told you that there is a pink elephant in the room with you right now, would you believe us? Probably not. There are no good reasons to believe that statement is true. Is faith in God just as crazy? Some people think so.

Scripture doesn't spend much time trying to convince people to believe in God's existence. To the original audience, the existence of God or gods was fairly uncontroversial. Biblical faith takes us beyond a simple belief in your head and moves deeper into an experience in your life. Hebrews 11:6 (NIV) says, "Without faith it is impossible to please God, because anyone who comes to him must believe that he exists and that he rewards those who earnestly seek him." Belief is a starting place, and it leads us to seek God in a relationship. Christianity is not just a belief that Jesus existed and died on the cross; it is accepting His sacrifice as the only cure for our sin problem. Christian faith is not about trusting in an idea; it's about trusting in a Person.

EVERYDAY FAITH

We walk by faith all the time. When was the last time you personally inspected an airplane before takeoff? When you take prescription medication, do you check your pharmacist's credentials? Can you even read the prescription your doctor wrote? You probably trusted the pilot, mechanics, doctor, and pharmacist without a second thought. Here's one way we like to define faith: Trusting what you do know in the face of what you don't know.

List five ways you practice faith in everyday life:

In the situations you listed above, what are some things that could go wrong ?

Knowing that there are always risks involved in faith, is it easy or difficult for you to trust people? Why?

A RELATIONSHIP OF FAITH

Why does a relationship with God require faith? In one sense, every relationship requires faith. Think of someone you believe loves you (a friend, a parent, a boyfriend or girlfriend, etc.). Now answer this question:

Why do you believe that person loves you? In the space provided, write out or draw what you think love is:

Author Gary Chapman has famously observed that we each receive and express love through five "Love Languages."[2] These love languages are 1) words of affirmation, 2) physical touch, 3) gifts, 4) quality time, and 5) acts of service. Circle the one in this list that you identify with most.

Is love something you can hold in your hand or look at under a microscope? What color is it? How much does it weigh? Love is not something you can see; it is something you can see expressed through people's actions and words—a shoulder to cry on, kind words, hugs and kisses, support and encouragement over many years, a helping hand. Your belief in love is built on faith based on your experiences.

Romans 5:8 says, "But God shows his love for us in that while we were still sinners, Christ died for us." God's love is not something we just invent or believe blindly; it is rooted in a historical event.[3] In fact, everyone (even atheists) must take a step of faith because nobody knows everything. We trust what we do know in the face of what we don't know.

THE GREAT BLONDIN!

Jean-Francois Gravelet (a.k.a. "The Great Blondin") was the first man to walk across Niagara Falls on a tightrope on June 30, 1859.[4] When he asked the crowd if they believed he could push a person in a wheelbarrow across the tightrope, they all agreed that he could. When he asked for a volunteer, everyone got really quiet! On another occasion, he carried a man on his back across the waterfall.[5] Who was the man? Blondin's long-time manager, Harry Colcord. Colcord knew Blondin. They had a relationship, which they built over many experiences, and this shared history gave him the confidence that he could trust Blondin with his life.

In a similar way, as we come to know God better through a relationship, we gain the confidence to trust Him, even when He calls us to step out and do scary things.

HOW FAITH GROWS

God may lead you into situations that require you to trust Him in order to grow your faith. In Exodus 14, the Egyptian army was behind the Israelites and a big body of water was in front of them. Either way they turned, they were trapped! They called out to God for help, and God replied to Moses, "Why do you cry to me? Tell the people of Israel to go forward" (Ex. 14:15). They did, and what happened next was one of the greatest miracles ever recorded: the waters parted for them. After they crossed to the other side, the Bible tells us, "Israel saw the great power that the LORD used against the Egyptians, so the people feared the LORD, and they believed in the LORD and in his servant Moses" (Ex. 14:31). They stepped out in faith, experienced a miracle of God's power, and then they came to trust God. They started with enough belief to cry out to God, but after facing their fears and obeying God's commands, their faith grew.

Are you ready to step forward with God so that He might grow your faith?

IN SUMMARY

- Without faith it is impossible to please God.
- Faith is not just about belief; it is about trusting a Person.
- Faith is trusting what we do know in the face of what we don't know.
- Our faith grows on the other side of obedience.

PREPARING FOR THE GROUP DISCUSSION

One thing that stood out to me today is:

One question I have based on today's study is:

CLOSING PRAYER

Thank You, God, that I can trust You in faith. Please give me the courage to move forward in obedience, no matter what "Red Sea" might be in front of me.

Encounters with God are God-Sized

"He did this so that all the peoples of the earth might know that the hand of the LORD is powerful and so that you might always fear the LORD your God."

JOSHUA 4:24 (NIV)

UNQUALIFIED (AND OKAY)

Have you ever felt totally unqualified to do something? If so, what was it?

Sometimes our lack of confidence is our own fault due to poor planning, like when I (Daniel) mixed-up the dates for a major oral report and had to hold a blank piece of paper and improvise. (It did not go well). Other times, we simply feel inadequate. We arrive at tryouts and quickly realize we're way outclassed. We may feel flustered after the first day of our new summer job. Many aspiring artists are reluctant to share their work out of fear that it's no good and they will be revealed as a fraud.

Have you ever decided not to do something due to a fear of failure (try out for a team, share the gospel with a classmate, apply for a job, speak up against abuse, etc.)? If so what was it?

GOODBYE, COMFORT ZONE

There is comfort in doing activities we're good at and avoiding ones we're not. Sometimes we take this same mindset into our relationship with God. Have you ever taken a test or inventory to determine what your gifts and talents are? We might assume that our skills and natural abilities determine how God wants us to serve Him. But God doesn't always operate that way in the Bible. Imagine that you're God and tasked with hiring for the following jobs.

Circle the most promising applicant.

Job: Lead an army of three hundred against a enemy of ten thousand.

Applicant 1: Battle-hardened and respected veteran general.

Applicant 2: Fearful man of lowly stature and little experience (last seen hiding in a pit).

Job: Parent the most important baby ever born.

Applicant 1: Experienced mother with money to access the best resources.

Applicant 2: Unmarried teen girl from a small town.

Job: Protest against a powerful king and then become the leader of a nation.

Applicant 1: Talented leader with sharp negotiating skills.

Applicant 2: A murderer with stuttering speech who is hiding in the desert.

In each of these Bible stories, God chose Applicant 2: Gideon (Judges 6–8), Mary (Luke 1:26-38), and Moses (Exodus 3–27).

> **Why do you think God used unconventional people to accomplish important tasks in the Bible?**

Earlier in this book, we talked about how God delights in inviting ordinary people to join His work. That news should excite us. But here's where things get a little scary—God doesn't call ordinary people to do ordinary things. God's mission is God-sized.

God doesn't just want you to do your best; He wants to accomplish His best through you. Christians need a faith built on a trusting relationship with God. Following Him will require us to leave our comfort zone, step out in faith, and attempt things we can't do in our own strength.

GLORY TO GOD

The battle of David and Goliath is one of the most famous stories in history. It is the classic underdog tale. Had a legendary hero killed Goliath in a long, epic, bloody battle, we would probably never have heard about it thousands of years later. For God to send a teenage shepherd without any armor against a nine-foot, battle-hardened giant would have seemed like a bad plan.

David knew how the situation looked, which is why he informed Goliath, "You come to me with a sword and with a spear and with a javelin, but I come to you in the name of the LORD of hosts, the God of the armies of Israel, whom you have defiled . . . that all the earth may know

Katie Davis was just a teenager when she moved to Uganda, adopted thirteen orphaned children, and launched Amazima Ministries.[6] She experienced far more than she could have ever imagined as she stepped out in faith and followed God one step at a time. You can read her story in her memoirs, *Kisses from Katie* and *Daring to Hope*.

that there is a God in Israel, and that all this assembly may know that the LORD saves not with sword and spear. For the battle is the LORD's, and he will give you into our hand" (1 Sam. 17:45-47).

The world is not impressed when they see Christians doing their best in the areas where they are naturally skilled. On the other hand, when God uses ordinary people to accomplish goals far bigger than themselves, others can't help but take notice. Our grandfather has said, "Our world is not seeing God, because we are not attempting anything that only God can do."

In the image below, list some of your strengths and talents within the circle. Next, in the space outside of the circle, list a few things that you think you can't do without God's strength and power.

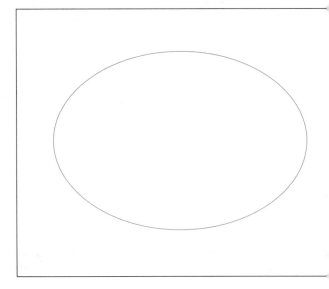

GOD-SIZED ENCOUNTERS

We need to be clear about two important facts.

1. "God-sized" encounters do not just involve us thinking big for God.

We shouldn't just try to brainstorm God-sized plans. We don't naturally know what He wants to do. The Holy Spirit will let us know what is on God's mind (1 Cor. 2:10-16). When you are obedient to follow Him, then you will become involved in His God-sized mission. We enter into a story that is much bigger than our own life.

2. "God-sized" may not always look big.

You might not need to sell everything you own, drop out of school, paradrop into the jungle, and live as a missionary in order to experience God-sized activity in your life. "God-sized" refers to something bigger than us that takes us beyond what is easy or natural for us to do without God's help. Is there a difficult or awkward classmate whom most people avoid? God-sized might simply mean showing that person the love of Jesus when nobody else is. Are you extremely shy and introverted? Good! God will receive the glory when you are obedient to speak up against injustice. Are all your friends doing things you know to be wrong? Ask God to help you be a light in the darkness and stand out as different.

Are you ready to let God do something through your life that is bigger than what you ever could do on your own?

IN SUMMARY

- Following God will require you to leave your comfort zone.
- God doesn't just want you to do your best; He wants to accomplish His best through you.
- God gets the glory when the world sees Christians doing things that only God can do.
- "God-sized" means bigger than us; something we need His help to accomplish.

PREPARING FOR THE GROUP DISCUSSION

One thing that stood out to me today is:

One question I have based on today's study is:

CLOSING PRAYER

Thank You, God, for not leaving me to live only on my own strength. Use my life this week to do something God-sized so everybody watching will see You.

Scared to Death

Humble yourselves, therefore, under the mighty hand of God so that at the proper time he may exalt you, casting all your anxieties on him, because he cares for you.

1 PETER 5:6-7

THE RED ROCKET

When I (Mike) was a teen, I remember driving my junky red minivan (affectionately known as "The Red Rocket") through our small town. Then, out of the corner of my eye, I saw my worst nightmare: a spider descending from the roof onto my shoulder! In the ensuing panic, I swerved across lanes as I desperately opened my door and flicked the horrifying creature outside. With the demon finally exorcised, I slammed the door shut and looked back to the road only to see that I was now facing an oncoming semi-truck. Thankfully, I was able to pull my van back into the proper lane before becoming a permanent hood ornament.

Our fears can be extremely distracting. The more we focus on our fears, the more our attention is taken away from things that really matter, and the results can be disastrous. When God calls us to take a step of faith and join Him in God-sized activity, we might be terrified. In fact, our grandfather has said, "If what God asks you to do doesn't scare you half to death, then you probably aren't hearing Him!"

THE FEAR FOOD CHAIN

Did you know that the Bible refers to fear 581 times?[7] It is not necessarily talking about things such as "Pogonophobia" (the fear of beards, which would have been an unfortunate phobia to have during biblical times). Instead of being a purely emotional state, the Bible often talks about fear as a form of wisdom.

A healthy fear can help you, but an unhealthy fear can hurt you. Wise people have their fears in the right order. Think of it as something like a "Fear Food Chain." A food chain is a pyramid with creatures at the top (humans) that eat everything else all the way down to the plants at the bottom. What if we put fears on the pyramid instead of foods?

Rank the following fears below in order of what you are most afraid of (1) to least afraid of (5):

____Being betrayed or let down by people I love

____Being laughed at or ridiculed

____Being alone or abandoned

____Being forced to do something I don't want to do

____Not knowing what the future holds for me

Write one sentence on why you picked the fear you did for number 1:

Write out one Bible verse that addresses the fear you picked for number 1:

GOOD FEARS AND BAD FEARS

Look at these verses on fear:

"Do not be anxious about anything, but in everything by prayer and supplication with thanksgiving let your requests be made known to God" (Phil. 4:6).

What does it mean to be anxious about something?

What do you get anxious about?

"The fear of the LORD is the beginning of wisdom, and the knowledge of the Holy One is insight" (Prov. 9:10).

Why is it wise to fear God?

If the Philippians verse tells us not to be anxious about anything and Proverbs tells us to fear God, is the Bible contradicting itself? What is the difference between being anxious and being fearful?

The Schramm T-130 is a huge drill used for digging wells. It is a powerful machine that can cause destruction and even death if you're not careful around it. But if you were one of the 33 Chilean miners who got trapped 2,300 feet under the earth in 2010, you would be forever grateful for this drill. After the miners had been trapped for sixty-nine days, the T-130 finally broke through the surface of the cave ceiling to rescue them.[8] The power that made them respect the T-130 is the very thing that led to their salvation.

POWER IN PERSPECTIVE

Respecting God properly is another way to think about fearing God. A healthy fear of God puts every other fear in perspective. Just like a food chain, the fear at the top (a healthy fear of God) "eats" all the others. Knowing God is all-powerful should lead to a healthy fear and respect, and this fear can also bring comfort.

The same power that causes us to fear God frees us from all other fears because He loves us. You don't have to fear loneliness, because this powerful God has promised never to leave you (Heb. 13:5). You don't have to fear what others think of you because your powerful Creator made you wonderful (Ps. 139:14). You don't have to fear the future because this powerful God has a plan for you (Eph. 2:10). A proper fear of God gives us a different perspective.

The Bible tells a story about Elisha and his servant being surrounded by an enemy army. The servant was terrified, but Elisha was calm. Then Elisha let his servant in on a little secret:

> [16] He said, "Do not be afraid, for those who are with us are more than those who are with them." [17] Then Elisha prayed and said, "O LORD, please open his eyes that he may see." So the LORD opened the eyes of the young man, and he saw, and behold, the mountain was full of horses and chariots of fire all around Elisha.
>
> 2 Kings 6:16-17

The God who was with them was far more powerful than anything else they were facing. The same is true for you.

Does this powerful God sit at the top of your "Fear Food Chain"?

IN SUMMARY

- Biblical fear isn't purely emotional; it has to do with wisdom.
- A healthy fear can help you, but an unhealthy fear can hurt you.
- We fear and respect God because of His power, but trust Him because of His love.
- A proper fear of God puts all other fears in perspective.

PREPARING FOR THE GROUP DISCUSSION

One thing that stood out to me today is:

One question I have based on today's study is:

CLOSING PRAYER

Thank You, God, that You are bigger than my fears. Please give me a proper fear of You, so that I can have wisdom to face every other fear in my life.

Faith Leads to Action

"Why do you call me 'Lord, Lord,' and not do what I tell you?"

Luke 6:46

DAY 4

FLAILING FALLS AND SOPRANO SCREAMS

I (Daniel) remember the summer we joined a group of fellow college students on a mission trip to Greece. One day as our bus was driving over the famous Corinth Canal, we saw a sign advertising bungee jumping. Beside it, mercifully, was a second sign that read "Closed."

"Too bad. I'd totally have done it and wouldn't have even screamed," I boasted.

"Me neither," added Mike. "I would have performed a perfect swan dive."

Several other guys added their own boasts. The girls in our group were undoubtedly impressed to be in the company of such brave and fearless men. Inside, we were all thanking God it was closed. Unfortunately for us, our local host overheard our chatter.

"Why didn't you say so!" he said. "I know the guy who works there. I'll give him a call." Before we could protest, he made the call, our bus turned around, and the jumpmaster arrived to open the site just for us. We soon found ourselves attached (with velcro!) to a flimsy bungee cord, standing on the edge of a bridge, and looking down at the water over two hundred feet below. After our heroic hot air, we had little choice. We jumped. I can neither confirm nor deny that I screamed in unbridled terror, but I do know that Mike's free fall more closely resembled a scared chicken than an elegant swan.

FAITH IN ACTION

We discovered that day (at the price of our dignity) that saying something and doing something are not the same. It's tempting to think of Christianity as just a list of beliefs about God and life.

What are five important ideas that you believe about God?

1. _____ 2. _____ 3. _____

4. _____ 5. _____

Having the right belief is certainly important. Jesus said, "Truly, truly, I say to you, whoever believes has eternal life" (John 6:47). But what does it mean to believe? Is it just thinking the right things in your head? Here's what James, Jesus's brother, had to say: "You believe that there is one God. Good! Even the demons believe that—and shudder" (James 2:19, NIV). He also wrote this:

> *14 What good is it, my brothers and sisters, if someone claims to have faith but has no deeds? Can such faith save them? 15 Suppose a brother or a sister is without clothes and daily food. 16 If one of you says to them, "Go in peace; keep warm and well fed," but does nothing about their physical needs, what good is it? 17 In the same way, faith by itself, if it is not accompanied by action, is dead.*

James 2:14-17, NIV

What is the difference between the belief Jesus was talking about that leads to eternal life (John 6:47) and the belief James was talking about that the demons have (James 2:19)?

What did James mean when he said that faith without action is dead?

James was not implying that belief is unimportant; he was saying that belief is the starting point of the Christian life, not the end point. It's important to keep faith and works in the proper order. Good works are the inevitable result of having the kind of faith James and Jesus described. All of our actions stem from what we believe.

Beliefs are invisible. You can't see, touch, hear, smell, or taste them. They exist inside our minds and hearts. When we explain our beliefs to someone with words, we are trying to give them a mental picture of what we think and feel. In contrast, our actions give a physical representation of what we believe. If we truly believe that God is real, that He is all-powerful, all-loving, and has a purpose for our lives, then these beliefs will be visible in the way we live.

FAITH BEYOND WORDS

We can say that we believe something, but our actions reveal what we really believe. In the safe company of Jesus and His close friends,

One reason why Christians are baptized is because it is a public display of faith. In baptism, a Christian takes the belief that they have professed with their words and demonstrates it through action. If you are a Christian but have not been baptized, we encourage you to talk to your parents and student pastor about it.

the disciple Peter brashly declared that even in the face of death he would never deny Jesus (Matt. 26:35). By the end of that same day, he had denied Jesus not once but three times. What he said he would do and what he actually did were two very different things.

Before we judge Peter too harshly, we should look at our own lives. Do we ever fail to back up the claims we make about God, faith, and morality? What does it look like to people outside the church when they observe Christians saying one thing with our mouths but something completely different with our actions? One study found that nearly eighty-five percent of young people outside the church thought that Christians were hypocritical.[9] They heard Christians talk one way but act another way.

Why are people bothered by hypocrisy?

Describe a time when your words and your actions did not match:

Now, describe a time when someone else's words and actions did not match. How did this experience make you feel?

The good news is that, just like Peter, God graciously gives us more chances to practice what we preach, even after we have messed up.

At the beginning of this day, we asked you to write down five things you believe about God. List them in the left column. Next, in the right column, list the ways that these beliefs might be demonstrated by your actions this week.

Belief 1:   *Action 1:*

Belief 2:   *Action 2:*

Belief 3:   *Action 3:*

Belief 4:   *Action 4:*

Belief 5:   *Action 5:*

We encourage you to put your beliefs and your words into action this week. Like the two of us in Greece, you're standing on the ledge looking down. Are you ready to make the jump?

IN SUMMARY

- Belief is the beginning, not the end, of the Christian life.
- Faith without action is dead.
- Our actions reveal what we truly believe.
- Hypocrisy harms our reputation as Christians, but God still shows us grace.

PREPARING FOR THE GROUP DISCUSSION

One thing that stood out to me today is:

One question I have based on today's study is:

CLOSING PRAYER

Thank You, God, for showing me grace even when my actions don't match my words. Please help me to put my faith into action this week.

WHILE YOU WATCH

As you watch the video, use the space provided to take notes or write down any thoughts and questions you have.

DISCUSSION

Based on what you learned in the video and in your personal Bible study days throughout the week, spend time discussing the questions below.

At the beginning of this week Mike shared how God helped him overcome his fear of becoming a pastor, as well as being diagnosed with type-1 diabetes.

What aspects of Mike's story do you relate to?

What fears do you have today?

Has God ever helped you overcome a fear in your life? Share an example with the group.

Mike and Daniel used the metaphor of bungee jumping to illustrate a leap of faith. This can be both exciting and terrifying.

Why can stepping out in faith sometimes be so scary?

What would help strengthen your belief?

Faith involves trust. Is it easy or difficult for you to trust people? Why or why not?

Although we like to think of ourselves as rational people, our beliefs are often far more influenced by our emotions and personal experiences. This can be dangerous since, as Jeremiah 17:9 warns us, "The heart is deceitful above all things, and desperately sick; who can understand it?"

How do your emotions or personal experiences affect what you believe?

Have your emotions or experiences ever led you to believe things that you later found out to be false or to reject something that you later found out to be true?

What are some ways you guard yourself from being deceived by your heart?

At the end of each day this week you wrote down one main takeaway and one question you had. Take turns sharing one of your takeaways or questions with the group.

GOING DEEPER

Faith is an essential part of being a Christian. Hebrews 11:6 says, "And without faith it is impossible to please him, for whoever would draw near to God must believe that he exists and that he rewards those who seek him." In the Biblical stories, people don't believe truths about God randomly. God reveals Himself to them in some way first.

Hebrews 11:1-40 is sometimes called the "Hall of Faith" because it lists biblical characters who each walked by faith in amazing ways. Below is a list of some of those characters, along with Bible verses that tell about their journey.

Choose one or more of these characters, read the corresponding verses, and then discuss the questions below. If you are in a larger group, you can split up into smaller groups and each take a name from the list to discuss, then come back together to share your thoughts with the rest of the group.

Abel	Hebrews 11:4; Genesis 4:1-16
Noah	Hebrews 11:7; Genesis 6:5-9; 7:1-5
Abraham	Hebrews 11:8-10; Genesis 12:1-9; 15:1-6
Sarah	Hebrews 11:11-12; Genesis 21:1-7
Joseph	Hebrews 11:22; Genesis 50:22-26
Moses and the Israelites	Hebrews 11:29; Exodus 14:15-22
Rahab	Hebrews 11:30-31; Joshua 2:8-14

What did God say to this person?

How did they put their faith into action?

What fears or difficulties did they overcome in order to step out in faith?

What did God do once they stepped out in faith?

What can you learn from them about your own faith journey?

PREVIEW VIDEO

Watch the short video introducing *Reality 6: Adjustments.*

PRAYER AND DISMISSAL

As a group, share any prayer requests and spend time in prayer. You may want to write these requests below as a reminder to pray for the people in your group throughout the week.

Adjustments

*But now, O L*ORD*, you are our Father; we are the clay, and you are our potter;*
we are all the work of your hand.

ISAIAH 64:8

And he said to all, "If anyone would come after me, let him deny himself
and take up his cross daily and follow me. For whoever would save his life
will lose it, but whoever loses his life for my sake will save it."

LUKE 9:23-24

"Now we have received not the spirit of the world, but the Spirit who is from
God, that we might understand the things freely given us by God."

1 CORINTHIANS 2:12

Little children, keep yourselves from idols.

1 JOHN 5:21

THE FINAL GAME OF A WASHED-UP LEGEND

I (Daniel) love hockey. During the Canadian winters, when the temperature plummeted, I enjoyed countless evenings playing on frozen ponds and on a local team. Sadly, increased responsibilities eventually led me to cut my "career" short. I met my girlfriend Sarah a few years after I stopped playing and later moved from Canada to South Carolina. At that point, I assumed she would never have the marvelous experience of witnessing me play hockey.

To my surprise, I discovered a hockey arena close by (perhaps the only one in the entire state), and I excitedly signed up for the recreational hockey league. Years without practice had dulled my skills (to put it mildly), and my athleticism had been eroded by my newfound appreciation for southern cooking, but I was confident that I could rediscover my long lost abilities before Sarah arrived in South Carolina.

When she finally visited, things got off to a perfect start. I proposed, and she said yes. What better way, I thought, to demonstrate what a catch she had just made than by letting her observe my hockey skills in action? The game was scheduled for the next evening, and what a game it was.

Both teams were tied at the end of regulation. Tension rose as we went to overtime, but neither team could get the upper hand. The contest would be decided in a glorious shootout. Save after save and goal after goal, our teams matched each other blow for blow until every player on both teams had participated in the shootout—except for one. This moment was my destiny.

I stepped over the bench and went to center ice. I looked to the stands where my new fiancé sat at the edge of her seat, her adoring gaze locked on me. The whistle blew, and I burst forward like a bullet. I envisioned myself completing a complex maneuver that would draw gasps of awe from the transfixed crowd. It would be the sort of goal that birthed legends. I was one fake into the sequence when my world was turned upside down—literally.

My skate got caught on the ice and I was launched through the air. I crashed back down to the ice, bouncing several times. My stick and other pieces of equipment left a trail behind me. My momentum carried me, face-down, all the way across the rink until I slammed against the end boards. It was not the beautiful goal I had envisioned.

I wanted to be a difference-making player in the game. I thought I would be prepared for those big moments without making any adjustments in my lifestyle, but I was wrong. As a result, I ended the night face-down in a heap instead of celebrating victory with my teammates.

The same is true when we participate in God's mission. We may love God and have good intentions, but unless we make the necessary adjustments (and allow God to make changes in us), we won't be prepared for what lies in front of us. This week we will look at *Reality 6: You must make adjustments in your life to join God in what He is doing.*

Are you ready to adjust your life to Him?

Changes

But now, O LORD, you are our Father; we are the clay,
and you are our potter;
we are all the work of your hand.

ISAIAH 64:8

INTO THE EDITING ROOM

Movies are an amazing art form. When we think of moviemaking, most of us picture a director standing behind a camera, yelling, "Lights! Camera! Action!" But according to those in the industry, much of the important work takes place behind the scenes. The late actor Phillip Seymour Hoffman (*Mission: Impossible III*, *The Hunger Games* trilogy) said, "The film is made in the editing room."[1] Similarly, Academy Award winning director Alejandro Gonzaelz Inarritu (*Birdman*, *The Revenant*) claimed, "Movies become art after editing."[2]

Directors gather hours upon hours of footage. They typically film dozens of takes of a single scene, allowing the actors to give slightly different performances. Then they go into the editing room and piece the film together like a complex puzzle. It is there that scenes or subplots are chopped, new elements are added in re-shoots, and the movie takes shape. There are many stories of filmmakers, amped up on coffee or energy drinks, still editing the film literally hours before it went to theaters, trying to get their creation "just right."

CHANGES

You are God's masterpiece (Eph. 2:10, 2 Cor. 5:17), but He is not finished with you yet. In order to fully experience the amazing purposes God has for your life, you must first allow yourself to enter the "editing room." Responding to God's invitation to join Him will require some adjustments in your life.

Circle any of the statements below that best describe you:

I love change.

I'm a creature of habit.

I'm satisfied with who
I currently am.

Change scares me.

I get bored when things stay the same.

I wish I could change things
about myself.

Think back on who you were two years ago. How similar or different are you today from who you were back then?

Based on your answer above, in what ways did your character change or grow?

If you could change three things about yourself, what would they be?

Experiencing God changes you. Paul said, "If anyone is in Christ, he is a new creation. The old has passed away; behold, the new has come" (2 Cor. 5:17). The Bible also uses a great metaphor of God as a potter and people as the clay (Isa. 64:8). If you've ever seen a potter work, it's pretty messy. By the time they are finished, the blob of clay has undergone an amazing transformation into something far more refined than how it started. God is your creator, and He knows what you can become if you allow Him to shape your life.

A DAILY COMMISSION

When Jesus called Simon (Peter) and Andrew to leave their fishing boats and become His disciples, He said, "Follow me, and I will make you fishers of men" (Matt. 4:19). Notice Jesus didn't say, "Follow me, and make yourselves fishers of men." Jesus was requesting their immediate obedience to follow Him, but He was also asking them to allow Him to work in their lives and make them into what He was calling them to be.

The message of the gospel isn't about what we can do for God but about what God does in and through us.

In 2 Corinthians 3:17-18, Paul wrote:

> [17] *Now the Lord is the Spirit, and where the Spirit of the Lord is, there is freedom.* [18] *And we all, with unveiled face, beholding the glory of the Lord, are being transformed into the same image from one degree of glory to another. For this comes from the Lord, who is Spirit.*

God is shaping our character to reflect Him more day by day.

In what ways might God shape your character to look more like Jesus?

How might God even use hardships or adversity to grow and shape us?

"Every block of stone has a statue inside it and it is the task of the sculptor to discover it."[3]

—Michelangelo

Based on extensive interviews, the sociologist Christian Smith famously coined the term "Moralistic Therapeutic Deism" to describe the kind of faith with which many young people were identifying.[4] Here's what he means. Moralistic: Try to be a good person. Therapeutic: Desire to be happy and comfortable. Deism: God is "out there" as creator, but not personally involved in our lives. Hopefully, over the course of this book, you've seen how this understanding of faith is not what God is calling us to; He has something much better for us.

A COTTAGE OR A PALACE?

We probably all want God to change us for the better. But how will you feel when the editing process is uncomfortable or even painful? Will you trust God if He asks you to cut something out of your life that you don't want to release? Perhaps He is telling you to break up with your boyfriend or girlfriend who is pressuring you to compromise your values or to quit the baseball team that requires you to miss church every Sunday. Will you trust God when He wants you to add something that scares you?

C.S. Lewis described it this way: Imagine that you are a "living house" and God comes to do some renovations. In the process, He begins knocking down walls or adding elements that we don't understand. Lewis wrote, "The explanation is that He is building quite a different house from the one you thought of—throwing out a new wing here, putting on an extra floor there, running up towers, making courtyards. You thought you were being made into a decent little cottage: but He is building a palace. He intends to come and live in it Himself."[5]

Over the next few days, we will look more specifically at different types of adjustments God may ask you to make. But before we do, you must determine whether you truly trust God to know best what "renovations" you need in your life.

In the space below, sketch out a blueprint for a house that represents your life. You can include rooms for your passions, habits, strengths, weaknesses, dreams, regrets, and so on.

How does it look? Now take a few moments to consider what areas God might need to add, expand, or remove from your house in order to remodel it into the palace He desires you to be.

Do you trust God enough to make the adjustments needed to follow Him?

IN SUMMARY

- You are God's masterpiece, but He isn't finished with you yet.
- Responding to God's invitation requires adjustments in your life.
- The gospel isn't about what you can do for God but about what God can do in and through you.
- When we put our faith in Jesus, God makes us a new creation.

PREPARE FOR THE GROUP DISCUSSION

One thing that stood out to me today is:

One question I have based on today's study is:

CLOSING PRAYER

God, thank You that You love me just as I am, but You also love me too much to keep me from growing. Please mold my life to look more like Jesus this week.

Rejecting Our Idols

Little children, keep yourselves from idols.

1 John 5:21

STUCK ON THE LADDER

One summer, I (Mike) spent some time roofing houses with my cousin. Shingles come in bundles that can weigh between fifty and eighty pounds. On one occasion, I was carrying a bundle on my shoulder up the ladder. When I tried to pass it to my cousin on the roof, it slipped and started sliding off the edge. We caught it together, stuck between the roof and the ladder. My cousin grabbed one end while facing down the roof, and I gripped the other while holding my ladder from tipping backward. The bundle was too heavy to get back on the roof, so we had a choice: let the shingles fall (and likely become damaged) or stay stuck on the ladder forever. In the interest of getting on with our lives, we let the shingles go.

LETTING GO

When it comes to experiencing God, we are in a similar position. There are all sorts of things we want to hold on to in our lives, but they prevent us from moving forward. Instead, we hang there stuck on the ladder, never climbing to where God desires for us to be.

The song "Let It Go" from the animated film *Frozen* struck a chord with people around the world. It sold millions of copies and won both a Grammy and an Academy Award. The basic premise of the song is that there are always things we need to give up if we want to experience something new. But there are some significant differences between Elsa's declarations and the biblical understanding of letting go. Hebrews 12:1 says, "Let us also lay aside every weight, and sin which clings so closely, and let us run with endurance the race that is set before us." This race is something God has laid out for us. While the famous Disney song is essentially an ode to self-empowerment and becoming our own gods, the biblical call on our lives is to sacrifice our selfishness and shed anything that keeps us from becoming what God desires for us to be.

IDOLS

What stands in our way is an idol problem.

What comes to mind when you think of the term "idol"?

Idols continually tripped up the Israelites during biblical times. Back then, idols were predominantly material creations that represented various gods. Scripture is full of warnings against worshiping idols (Ex. 20:3-6; Lev. 19:4; 1 Cor. 10:14; 1 John 5:21; Rev. 9:20). At its core, worshiping an idol is simply replacing God with anything that is not God. An idol becomes the most important thing to us. It takes our time, energy, and money. We think about it constantly. We worry about losing it, and we ultimately allow it to shape how we act. Why? Because we love it. It gives our lives meaning. Author Timothy Keller said that every sin reveals an idol in our lives. In fact, the human heart is an "idol factory."[6] When we commit the sin of jealousy, we have made an idol of what the other person has that we wish we had. When we gossip, we show that we have idolized popularity, which leads us to tear others down to build ourselves up.

Match the sins in the left hand column with the idols in the right hand column below.

Sins	Idols
Jealousy	Popularity
Gossip	Fairness
Greed	Our Appearance
Putting another relationship in place of God	Entertainment and leisure
Harming our bodies	The newest phone
Pornography	Sex
Laziness	A boyfriend or girlfriend
Revenge	Someone who has what we want

THE RICH YOUNG RULER

Take a few minutes to read the story in Luke 18:18-27. You may feel like you don't identify with this guy, but perhaps you can relate more than you realize. He was young. If you live in the United States or Canada, then you are likely rich compared to most of the world. And social media has given us a platform to reach and influence hundreds more people than many rulers in ancient times could have imagined. What Jesus said to him also applies to us.

When the young man approached Jesus, he was looking for eternal life. In John 17:3, Jesus said, "And this is eternal life, that they know you, the only true God, and Jesus Christ whom you have sent." What the young man was searching for could only be found in experiencing a relationship with God through Jesus Christ.

Jesus eventually told the man to give away his wealth and follow Him. His possessions were the "weight" keeping him from running the race set before him (Heb. 12:1). The young man thought he was doing everything right by keeping the commandments, but did you notice

The singing competition *American Idol* is one of the most successful TV shows of all time. In many ways, idols are exactly what the show was designed to create: someone in the spotlight to be watched, cheered, followed, copied, paid, and (arguably) worshiped by millions of fans around the world. There are many other less obvious forms of idol worship around us. Can you think of some?

"My desire for acceptance is one of the crosses that I carry. Each morning I have to attend a funeral. My own. I have to wake up and once again die to my desires for people's approval."

—Lecrae[7]

which commandments Jesus didn't mention? He left out the command against having idols. Jesus didn't tell him; He showed him. When the young man couldn't give up his wealth, it became obvious exactly what his idol was.

YOUR IDOLS

Buddhism claims that our selfish desires are the problem. One common story tells of a man approaching Buddha and claiming, "I want happiness," to which Buddha replied, "First remove 'I,' that's Ego, then remove 'want,' that's Desire. See now you are left with only 'Happiness.'" Christianity, however, claims that the problem with our desires is that they are misplaced. The things we desire take the place of God and can become objects of our worship.

As C.S. Lewis put it, "If we find ourselves with a desire that nothing in this world can satisfy, the most probable explanation is that we were made for another world … If that is so, I must take care, on the one hand, never to despise, or be unthankful for, these earthly blessings, and on the other, never to mistake them for the something else of which they are only a kind of copy, or echo, or mirage."[8]

What three things in your life are you tempted to make idols?

In what ways do each of these hold you back from following Jesus? Explain how in the space below.

Idol 1   How it holds me back

Idol 2   How it holds me back

Idol 3   How it holds me back

We cannot hold onto our idols and follow Jesus at the same time. Are you ready to let go of the idols in your life?

"Is there any hope? Yes, if we begin to realize that idols cannot simply be removed. They must be replaced. If you only try to uproot them, they grow back; but they can be supplanted. By what? By God himself, of course."[9]

—Timothy Keller

IN SUMMARY

- Idols are anything we put in the place of God.
- At the root of every sin is an idol.
- We chase after idols because deep down we love them.
- If we want to follow Jesus, we must leave our idols behind.

PREPARING FOR THE GROUP DISCUSSION

One thing that stood out to me today is:

One question I have based on today's study is:

CLOSING PRAYER

God, You are greater than anything else I am tempted to worship in Your place. Please guard my heart from turning even good things into idols.

Positive Adjustments

And he said to all, "If anyone would come after me, let him deny himself and take up his cross daily and follow me. For whoever would save his life will lose it, but whoever loses his life for my sake will save it."

Luke 9:23-24

DAY 3

OUT WITH THE OLD, IN WITH THE NEW

I (Daniel) loved few things as much as my green Teenage Mutant Ninja Turtles t-shirt. A sentimental birthday gift from my girlfriend, the shirt was uncommonly comfortable, fit me perfectly, and I was convinced it was lucky. I wore it more often than was hygienically appropriate. After several years, the shirt's vibrant green color developed a hue of murky swamp water, the image on the front was faded beyond recognition, and the once-comfortable fabric had the consistency of cheap tissue paper. None of these issues deterred me from wearing my cherished shirt with pride—until the unthinkable and unfortunate happened.

I sensed it as soon as I arrived home. I rushed to my bedroom, and my worst fears were confirmed. There was a TMNT shirt-sized gap in my closet (and my heart). As a public service to society, the gift-giver (now my wife) had thrown the shirt in the garbage. It was gone forever, and I started my journey through the five stages of grief. The next day, my wife surprised me with a gift. I opened the bag and pulled out a brand new TMNT shirt—greener, more comfortable, and destined to be even luckier than the old shirt had ever been. Never had I loved a gift (or a gift-giver) more!

As God makes the appropriate adjustments in our lives, there will be idols we need to remove. But the goal is not to empty ourselves completely. Rather, these adjustments will make room for other, far better things.

Read the verses quoted at the top of this page (Luke 9:23-24). Notice the pattern for being a disciple of Jesus. We remove our selfishness ("deny himself") and replace it with our commitment to Him ("take up his cross daily"), which leads to experiencing Jesus and His plans for us ("follow me").

What might these adjustments look like in our lives?

ADJUSTMENTS IN OUR THINKING

We are naturally selfish, so fulfilling Jesus's command to deny ourselves will certainly require changes in the ways we think. Romans 12:2 says, "be transformed by the renewal of your mind." An encounter with Jesus will lead to changes in our thoughts.

Acts 10:9-33 tells an interesting story. At that time, the Jewish people viewed non-Jews (Gentiles) as "unclean" and tried to avoid them. God gave the disciple Peter a vision that clearly revealed some adjustments that needed to take place in the way Peter viewed Gentiles. Peter explained it this way: "You yourselves know how unlawful it is for a Jew to associate with or to visit anyone of another nation, but God has shown me that I should not call any person common or unclean" (v. 28). Jesus's death on the cross was for anyone who would accept it, whether or not they were a Jew or a Gentile (Gal. 3:28). Based on that truth, Peter was going to have to start thinking differently about people who were different from him.

How might God lead you to change your thinking? Use the examples below to think through different situations where Jesus has called us to change our thinking.

Example 1: Someone at school is treating you badly, but you read that Jesus said to "love your enemies" (Matt. 5:44).

How might being a disciple of Jesus change the way you view this person?

Example 2: You are busy making plans for after you graduate from high school, but then you read, "For my thoughts are not your thoughts, neither are your ways my ways, declares the LORD. For as the heavens are higher than the earth, so are my ways higher than your ways and my thoughts than your thoughts" (Isa. 55:8-9).

How does your relationship with God change the way you plan for the future?

Example 3: You hate school (or perhaps just certain classes). Or maybe you can't stand your part-time job. Then you read Colossians 3:23, "Whatever you do, work heartily, as for the Lord and not for men."

How does knowing that Jesus is your Lord change the way you think about school and work when they're not enjoyable?

Much of the purpose of modern technology is to save us time by allowing us to multitask. Ironically, multitasking actually makes us less efficient by continuing to add more into our lives, instead of taking things away. It has been found to increase stress, make our brains more foggy, and even cause us to become addicted to the habit of losing focus![9]

Media can easily consume our lives. One study found that teens (ages 13-18) spent almost nine hours per day consuming some form of entertainment media (TV, video games, social media, music, etc.).[10] These things aren't necessarily bad (especially something like reading a book), but that's still a lot going into our brains. How often during the day are you simply still with your own thoughts?

ADJUSTMENTS IN OUR ACTIONS

How we think affects how we act. Like a chiropractor slowly adjusting our spine back into alignment, the changes God leads us through will put us in a better position to live the way He designed us to live.

Example 1: You've never really made time to read your Bible, but then someone shares this verse with you: "All Scripture is breathed out by God and profitable for teaching, for reproof, for correction, and for training in righteousness, that the man of God may be complete, equipped for every good work" (2 Tim. 3:16-17).

How can regularly reading the Bible lead to positive changes in your life? What adjustments could you make to read or listen to God's Word regularly?

Example 2: You've gotten out of the habit of going to church. Or maybe you attend, but you're just a passive observer, not an active participant. One day you come across these verses: "And let us consider how to stir up one another to love and good works, not neglecting to meet together, as is the habit of some, but encouraging one another, and all the more as you see the Day drawing near" (Heb. 10:24-25).

What changes could you make in how you express love and good works both at church and in other areas of your life?

Example 3: You and your friends plan to binge watch a show that you know contains a lot of questionable content, then you remember Psalm 101:2-4: "I will ponder the way that is blameless … I will walk with integrity of heart within my house; I will not set before my eyes anything that is worthless. I hate the work of those who fall away; it shall not cling to me. A perverse heart shall be far from me; I will know nothing of evil."

How might these verses change the way you make entertainment decisions?

There are many other adjustments God might lead us to make along the way. As we leave our idols behind to follow Him, God will introduce new things into our lives that are aligned with His will.

Are you ready to make the proper adjustments?

IN SUMMARY

- God removes the wrong things in our lives so He can add the right things.
- Being a disciple of Jesus requires us to leave behind our selfishness and follow Him.
- Following Jesus will lead to adjustments in the ways we think.
- Following Jesus will lead to adjustments in the ways we act.

PREPARING FOR THE GROUP DISCUSSION

One thing that stood out to me today is:

One question I have based on today's study is:

CLOSING PRAYER

Thank You, God, that the changes You have for my life are good for me. Please show me the adjustments You want me to make.

One Step at a Time

"His master replied, 'Well done, good and faithful servant! You have been faithful with a few things; I will put you in charge of many things. Come and share your master's happiness!'"

Matthew 25:23 (NIV)

THE POWER OF SMALL CHANGES

Great Britain was once the laughingstock of competitive cycling. In a span of a hundred years, they won just one Olympic gold medal, and no Brit had ever won the Tour de France (cycling's biggest race). Their reputation was so bad that a bike manufacturer actually stopped selling them bikes, worried sales would suffer if people saw the British team using their gear. Then Dave Brailsford became the performance director and everything changed. His philosophy was simple: think of everything that goes into riding a bike and improve it by just one percent. They targeted even seemingly insignificant areas, such as the pillows they used, the way they washed their hands, and the color of their bikes.

Guess what? It worked. Five years later, they won eight Olympic gold medals. Four years after that, they set nine Olympic records. In a span of just ten years, the British cyclists won an astonishing 178 world championships, 66 Olympic and Paralympic gold medals, and had five Tour de France victories.[11] One of the most dominant stretches in cycling history came by improving every day by just one percent.

FAITHFUL IN A LITTLE

Have you ever made an ambitious new commitment or resolution that started well, but didn't last? What was it?

What caused you to stop pursuing that goal?

New Year's resolutions have become an ongoing joke because we rarely actually keep them (around eighty percent of resolutions fail).[12] Perhaps the primary reason for our failure is because we typically desire instant gratification. We want to get into better physical shape, but after a few days sweating in the gym without seeing noticeable changes, we quit. We want to do better at school, but we grow tired of studying, so we settle for a lower grade. We'd love to be a more competent musician, but can't seem to find time to practice, so we stop improving. We can also take this mindset into how we view God.

Why do we grow discouraged when our good intentions to grow in our faith don't happen?

Who is an example of someone in your life who inspires you to deepen your relationship with God?

For us, one person who inspires us is our grandfather. He has traveled around the world, spoken to massive crowds, and even been invited to the White House. Growing up, we would look at his life and think, "We want God to use our lives too, but we will never have the level of faith or close relationship with God that he has." Here is an important lesson we've learned: when our grandfather was our age, he wasn't a spiritual superhero either! But as a teenager, he committed to wake up early enough to pray and read his Bible each morning. He continued to make small adjustments in his life day after day, year after year. Those adjustments added up over time.

To become the person that God desires you to be requires commitment and patience. The Bible says, "If you are faithful in little things, you will be faithful in large ones. But if you are dishonest in little things, you won't be honest with greater responsibilities" (Luke 16:10, NLT). There is no healthy shortcut to growth, as I (Mike) found out when I dumped a whole pack of fertilizer on my basil plant. The next day, it was scorched and more closely resembled the barren surface of Mars than the lush garden of Eden!

God chooses to grow us through small things to prepare us to join Him in bigger ones. Think of the story of David and Goliath. Did David go from humble shepherd boy to mighty warrior facing down a giant overnight? Not at all. Day after day, David had learned to trust God with smaller threats like wild animals (1 Sam. 17:34-36). When the time came to protect God's people from a large threat, David was ready for the task. He was able to claim with confidence, "The LORD who delivered me from the paw of the lion and from the paw of the bear will deliver me from the hand of this Philistine" (1 Sam. 17:37). David's experience in the shepherd's field prepared him for his encounter on the battlefield.

The classic Star Wars movie, *The Empire Strikes Back*, includes a famous scene where Luke Skywalker attempts to lift his crashed spaceship out of the swamp using the Force—the movie's version of spirituality. Unsuccessful, he exclaims, "I can't, it's too big!" His little green master, Yoda, informs him, "Size matters not." Confused, Luke responds, "Master, moving stones around is one thing, but this is totally different!"[13] What he failed to realize was that the same power that could move the small things could also move the big things. The problem was that Luke did not yet have the faith to believe it. In a similar way, God is capable of doing big things in our lives, but He grows our faith with the smaller "stones" first.

TRAINING

The Bible frequently compares the Christian life to the life of an athlete. Here is how the apostle Paul described it:

> *24 Do you not know that in a race all the runners run, but only one gets the prize? Run in such a way as to get the prize. 25 Everyone who competes in the games goes into strict training. They do it to get a crown that will not last, but we do it to get a crown that will last forever. 26 Therefore I do not run like someone running aimlessly; I do not fight like a boxer beating the air. 27 No, I strike a blow to my body and make it my slave so that after I have preached to others, I myself will not be disqualified for the prize.*

1 Corinthians 9:24-27

I (Daniel) have always enjoyed running, but for years I was too intimidated to try longer runs. I had never run more than three miles, so how could I ever run a 26.2-mile marathon? It wasn't until our little sister encouraged me to register for a race that I finally committed to try. What I learned was that I wasn't actually increasing my distance from three to twenty-six miles. I was increasing it from three to three and a half, then to four, then from four to five, adding distance little-by-little over several months until I could run 26.2 miles. The key was not to get overwhelmed by the end goal but to focus instead on getting a little bit better every day.

There is a famous movie troupe called "The Training Montage." You've probably seen it, often in martial arts movies (*Karate Kid, Mulan, Kung Fu Panda*) or sports movies (*Rocky, Creed*). The characters go through a time of training and learning in order to move them from where they are to where they need to be. The whole point of the montage is to condense for us (the viewers) what inevitably takes longer for the characters. Why? Because growth is not instantaneous; it takes time.

Some adjustments might need to be drastic and immediate (ending a sexually impure relationship, immoral habits, etc.), while others may require more gradual adjustments (becoming a more encouraging person, having a more vibrant prayer life, etc.). God loves you as you are, but He also desires for you to grow. How can you be more intentional about this growth?

Review the Spiritual Growth Training Plan example below and create your on the next page.

Area of Growth	Immediate Adjustment	Gradual Adjustment	Action Plan	Accountability
Biblical Understanding	Order a new Bible in a good translation.	Commit to reading at least one chapter a day before school, five days a week.	1. Create a checklist to print out and keep on the nightstand. 2. Join a Bible study at church.	Ask my youth leader to check in on my progress every Sunday.

What about you? Choose 1-3 areas of growth and begin to develop a plan. You may want to take a picture of this chart to keep yourself accountable.

Area of Growth	Immediate Adjustment	Gradual Adjustment	Action Plan	Accountability

IN SUMMARY

- Spiritual growth takes time.
- Small adjustments add up over time and lead to big change.
- God prepares you for bigger tasks by growing your faith in smaller ones.
- Spiritual growth takes discipline, dedication, and accountability.

PREPARE FOR THE GROUP DISCUSSION

One thing that stood out to me today is:

One question I have based on today's study is:

CLOSING PRAYER

God, thank You for Your patience with me. Give me the wisdom and perseverance to pick up my cross daily and follow You.

WHILE YOU WATCH

As you watch the video, use the space provided to take notes or write down any thoughts and questions you have.

DISCUSSION

Based on what you learned in the video and in your personal Bible study days throughout the week, spend time discussing the questions below.

Mike and Daniel shared this week that you are an unfinished masterpiece.

How does this affect the way you see yourself?

How does this affect the way you understand your relationship with God?

What are some changes God has done in your life over the last two years?

Often, when we are misaligned with God, it is because we have chosen to follow after an idol instead of Him. (An idol can be anything that takes the place of God in our lives.)

What are some idols in our culture?

What are some idols that are tempting for you to follow?

How has God helped you leave your idols behind?

As God changes you as a Christian, how should you start to think and act differently from the world around you?

At the end of each day this week you wrote down one main takeaway and one question you had. Take turns sharing one of your takeaways or questions with the group.

GOING DEEPER

As you respond to God's invitation to join Him at work in the world, you will need to make adjustments in your life. These adjustments involve both addition and subtraction. There are aspects of your character, thoughts, and actions that God will remove, and also things God wants to add.

No matter how hard we try, the truth is that we'll never be able to make enough changes in our lives to measure up to the goodness God has called us to. The good news is that the Holy Spirit can make those changes in us. Look at the contrast Paul made in Galatians 5:16-25 between living life apart from God ("the flesh") and living according to what the Holy Spirit can do in us.

> [16] But I say, walk by the Spirit, and you will not gratify the desires of the flesh. [17] For the desires of the flesh are against the Spirit, and the desires of the Spirit are against the flesh, for these are opposed to each other, to keep you from doing the things you want to do. [18] But if you are led by the Spirit, you are not under the law. [19] Now the works of the flesh are evident: sexual immorality, impurity, sensuality, [20] idolatry, sorcery, enmity, strife, jealousy, fits of anger, rivalries, dissensions, divisions, [21] envy, drunkenness, orgies, and things like these. I warn you, as I warned you before, that those who do such things will not inherit the kingdom of God. [22] But the fruit of the Spirit is love, joy, peace, patience, kindness, goodness, faithfulness, [23] gentleness, self-control; against such things there is no law. [24] And those who belong to Christ Jesus have crucified the flesh with its passions and desires. [25] If we live by the Spirit, let us also keep in step with the Spirit.

Which of the sins listed by Paul are the most prominent in our culture today? Why?

In what ways do the "works of the flesh" destroy our relationship with God and with other people?

What might the "fruit" of the Spirit that Paul lists look like in your life?

Which of these "fruit of the Spirit" does the world need more of? Which of them do you want more of in your own life?

As the Holy Spirit works to change us from the inside, Jesus also calls us to make some changes in our lives. In Luke 9:23-24, Jesus described what it means to follow after Him and be His disciple:

> 23 And he said to all, "If anyone would come after me, let him deny himself and take up his cross daily and follow me. 24 For whoever would save his life will lose it, but whoever loses his life for my sake will save it.

Why do you think Jesus established these radical standards for His followers?

What does it mean to "deny" yourself? Why is this so difficult for us?

Is there a difference between denying yourself and taking up your cross daily? If so, what is the difference?

What do you think Jesus meant by the surprising statement: "For whoever would save his life will lose it, but whoever loses his life for my sake will save it"?

Together as a group, brainstorm answers to the questions below for the three areas of adjustments. If you are a larger group, you may also divide into three smaller groups, have each group take one of the areas, and then join back together to share afterwards.

In what way(s) should I "deny myself" in this area?

In what way(s) should I "take up my cross" in this area?

In what way(s) can I "follow" Jesus in this area?

Thoughts   *Actions*   *Character*

PREVIEW VIDEO

Watch the short video introducing *Reality 7: Experiencing God.*

PRAYER & DISMISSAL

As a group, share any prayer requests and spend time in prayer. You may want to write these requests below as a reminder to pray for the people in your group throughout the week.

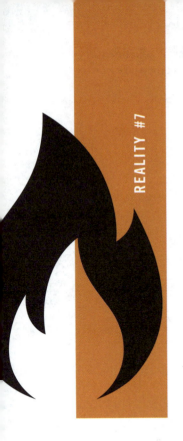

Experiencing God

"I had heard of you by the hearing of the ear, but now my eye sees you."

JOB 42:5

"Truly, truly, I say to you, whoever believes in me will also do the works that I do; and greater works than these will he do, because I am going to the Father."

JOHN 14:12

"You are my friends if you do what I command you."

JOHN 15:14

I have been crucified with Christ. It is no longer I who live, but Christ who lives in me. And the life I now live in the flesh I live by faith in the Son of God, who loved me and gave himself for me.

GALATIANS 2:20

6,931 MILES AND 65 YEARS

Gerald Richard Sanders, originally from England, was a banker in Canada. When World War I swept across Europe, he enlisted as a machine gunner in the Canadian armed forces. He could have died many times. On one occasion, he excused himself for a short bathroom break and was replaced at his gun by a good friend. When he returned, there was a bomb crater where his station had been. He never forgot his best friend's sacrifice.

Eventually, the war ended, and he moved with his family to Prince Rupert, Canada, just south of the Alaska border. It was a rough mining town with no church. Although G.R.S. was a banker with no training as a pastor, he sensed God wanted him to start a church for his family. So, he joined God in His work. Every Sunday morning he would rent an old dance hall, and they would worship together. His wife played the piano, he preached, and their three sons would join them.

For six months the church consisted of only their family. This could easily have become discouraging. Was God even at work in this forgotten town in the middle of nowhere? Was their little family on God's radar? Then one day a stranger slipped in the back during their Sunday morning service. His life had been devastated by alcohol abuse, and he'd lost his job, his marriage, and his family as a result. He was actually on his way to end his life by jumping off a bridge on the outskirts of town. As the man had been walking, he heard music coming from the dance hall and slipped in to check it out. After hearing G.R.S. present the good news of Jesus, this man surrendered his life to Christ. From that point on, the church started to grow.

We didn't tell you G.R.S.'s last name. It was Blackaby, and he was our great-grandfather. The story doesn't end there.

When I (Mike) was a teenager, I traveled with my dad to Qatar in the Middle East. Dad preached at an international church on Sunday, and he told the story of G.R.S. faithfully starting that church. At the end of the service, a young couple excitedly approached him. "We have to tell you something," they exclaimed. "That church your grandfather started still exists today. In fact, we came to know Jesus and were married in that church!"

Wow. We were in a different country 6,931 miles away from that Canadian town, and we were meeting a couple who had entered into a relationship with God (and each other) in that same church. Sixty-five years later, our great-grandfather's faithfulness was still impacting people.

What can God do through your life? Anything He wants, if you let Him. The impact you can have just by being faithful to join God in His activity can have a ripple effect that continues long after we are gone. Our great-grandfather wasn't a superhero; he was simply faithful one day at a time. In this chapter, we'll look at the final reality of Experiencing God. *Reality 7: We come to experience God as we obey Him and He accomplishes His purposes through us.*

Knowledge and Experience

"I had heard of you by the hearing of the ear, but now my eye sees you."

Job 42:5

DAY 1

A FUTURE PALEONTOLOGIST

When our friend was a kid, he was really into dinosaurs. His favorite movie was obviously *Jurassic Park*. He had all the toys and could tell you endless facts about each and every character or dinosaur in the film. He was a walking Jurassic encyclopedia. But when we asked him how many times he had watched Spielberg's classic, he quickly replied, "Oh, I've never seen it. It's too scary for me!"

There is a huge difference between knowing about something in your head and experiencing it firsthand. You can read books, hear stories, and watch documentaries about surfing, roller coasters, music, and good food, but there is no substitute for having the experience for yourself.

What is a new experience that you hope to have one day? Why?

Describe an experience (good or bad) that turned out to be very different from how you imagined it would be:

In what ways did your knowledge change based on your experience?

The Bible tells of a group of religious leaders who had Jesus right in front of them but refused to believe that He was the Son of God. Instead, they occupied themselves with studying Scripture and attempting to obey every religious law to be pure before God. Jesus challenged them, "You search the Scriptures because you think that in them you have eternal life; and it is they that bear witness about me, yet you refuse to come to me that you may have life" (John 5:39-40). They were filling their heads with knowledge and study, but they missed out on a relationship with Jesus—the very person their Scriptures foretold.

THE PROBLEM OF PAIN

Our experiences are complicated. If we're not careful, they may confuse our understanding of God. This confusion is especially evident when it comes to something called "The Problem of Pain," which, in short, asks the question, "If God is all-powerful and all-loving, why does He allow suffering in the world?" Generations of theologians, philosophers, and hipsters at Starbucks have debated this massive question. Here are a few thoughts to consider:

1. Freedom of Choice

Do you believe love is a good thing? Is love possible if it is forced? You may love your phone, but if Siri says, "I love you too," it's because she has been programmed to respond that way. You may love your pet, but do animals truly love us back the same way humans do? Humans are unique in our ability to choose love, but our freedom can be used for good or evil, and poor choices lead to much (though not all) of the pain we see around us. Why doesn't God just intervene when people are about to make a poor choice? Do you like it when people override your choices? Likely not, yet we often assume that we'd be okay with God doing exactly that.

> List three possible reasons why God might not always intervene to stop painful circumstances:

2. Limited Experience

We are driven primarily by our emotions. Psychologist Jonathan Haidt uses the metaphor of an elephant rider. The rider is our logical, rational self, and there is only so much he can do to steer the emotional beast he is riding.[1] We may feel one thing today and something completely different tomorrow. Our understanding of truth cannot swing back and forth with our emotions. We need an anchor to ground our beliefs. Rather than determining who God is based exclusively on our experiences, we should understand our experiences through the lens of who God is. The rider and the elephant must work together to give us a more complete picture of the world.

> Think of a painful experience in your life. How did your emotions influence the way you understood God and His goodness at the time?

3. God is with us in our suffering.

Jesus promised His disciples, "And I will ask the Father, and he will give you another Helper, to be with you forever" (John 14:16). That Helper (the Holy Spirit) lives in you if you are a believer in Jesus, which means you never face pain alone. Jesus knows what it is like to suffer (Heb. 2:18), so He understands what you're going through. He doesn't just have sympathy for you ("Wow, that must be hard!"); He has empathy ("I know what that feels like.").

> Describe a time when a painful experience actually brought you closer to God:

VALLEYS, SLOPES, AND SUMMITS

We grew up near the Rocky Mountains. Regardless of how big or small they are, all mountains have the same three features: valleys, slopes, and a summit.

Think of your life as traveling through a mountain range. There will be difficult valleys and inspiring summits. Most of life, however, is lived on the slopes in between these two extremes. Your experience (and your perspective of your surroundings) differs depending on where you are standing on the mountain.

UP, DOWN, AND BACK UP AGAIN

The great prophet Elijah was well-acquainted with mountains, and they often seemed to reflect the conditions of his life. At the top of Mount Carmel, he experienced a miraculous victory in a "spiritual duel" against 950 pagan prophets when God sent blazing fire from heaven (1 Kings 18:16-45). Then the wicked queen Jezebel threatened to kill him, so Elijah fled in fear to the valley. God met him there, at his lowest point, and helped him to move forward to another mountain. After Elijah climbed the slopes, God revealed the great plans that still lay ahead for him. The valleys in Elijah's life humbled him to lean on God's strength; the slopes made him work to move forward, and the summits inspired him for the future. All parts of the mountain helped him to grow as a person.

What is one thing that we can learn or benefit from in each of these experiences?

The Valleys of Life: _____

The Slopes of Life: _____

The Summits of Life: _____

Go back and mark on the mountain above where you think you currently are in your life. Write out one way you can continue to move forward through the mountain range, regardless of where you are:

IN SUMMARY

- There is a big difference between head-knowledge and personal experience.
- Painful experiences can cloud or clarify our understanding of God.
- Life is made up of valleys, slopes, and summits.
- Wherever you are on the mountain, good can come from it.

PREPARING FOR THE GROUP DISCUSSION

One thing that stood out to me today is:

One question I have based on today's study is:

CLOSING PRAYER

Thank You, God, that You want me to experience You in my life, not just know about You in my head. Please help me to get the most out of whatever part of the mountain I am currently on.

Obedience

"You are my friends if you do what I command you."

John 15:14

DAY 2

PEANUT BUTTER HEAD

I (Mike) bought a puppy that my oldest son named Chewie (yes, from *Star Wars*). One day he got into our recycle bin while in the backyard and found a large peanut butter container. He poked his little head inside to see if there was anything left and got stuck. Chewie panicked and began running blindly around the yard, smashing into chairs, fences, and toys. The whole family kept calling to him, commanding him to stop, but the dog wouldn't listen. Thankfully, a well-timed tackle finally halted the spazzy canine, and we managed to pull the container off his head.

The longer Chewie ignored our commands, the more banged up and disoriented he became. It's easy to understand giving a dog commands for his own benefit, but when it comes to us receiving commands, we get a little more defensive.

TO OBEY OR NOT TO OBEY?

Obedience can be a difficult word for us to accept. It makes us feel like children being bossed around. In the worst cases, obedience may even remind us of abuse.

What thoughts and feelings does the word "obedience" bring up in your mind and heart? Why?

Why do you think the idea of obedience often has negativity attached to it?

In what areas of your life (family, school, sports, etc.) do you struggle the most with being obedient?

Despite the negative stigma, we actually practice obedience all the time. We don't shoplift, because we obey the store rules; we follow our parents' curfews; we drive the speed limit; we turn in our assignments before the deadline; we run laps when our coach tells us to. Obedience can be good or bad depending on who you're obeying.

What does obeying God look like?

BIBLICAL OBEDIENCE

The Bible is full of verses on obedience to God (Deut. 5:33; Psalm 128:1; Ez. 20:19-20; Luke 10:27; James 1:22). Jesus said, "You are my friends if you do what I command you" (John 15:14). Obedience is an important part of being a Christian, but obeying rules and laws isn't what makes us a Christian. Romans 5:19 tells us, "For as by the one man's disobedience the many were made sinners, so by the one man's obedience the many will be made righteous." Paul was comparing the lives of Adam (the first human, representing all of us) and Jesus. He said that Adam's disobedience led to sin, but because Jesus perfectly obeyed God the Father in our place, by His obedience we are made right before God.

OBEDIENCE AS A RESPONSE

We do not obey God in an attempt to earn His love because He has already given it. Before God gave His people the famous Ten Commandments, He first rescued them from slavery in Egypt. This is why the Ten Commandments begin like this: "I am the LORD your God, who brought you out of the land of Egypt, out of the house of slavery" (Ex. 20:2). In a similar way, Jesus has proven His love for us on the cross and rescued us from the slavery of sin (Rom. 6:20-21).

Is there anyone in your life that you don't mind listening to and doing things for? Why is this?

Is there someone in your life you struggle to obey? Why?

What is the difference between being forced to obey and choosing to obey?

In the dystopian book series, *The Hunger Games*, the powerful President Snow requires all twelve districts to send one young man and one young woman to compete in a battle to the death each year as "tributes." Eventually, the districts rise up in a rebellion led by Katniss Everdeen and refuse to obey the barbaric rules of an evil system.

SURRENDER

Hiroo Onada was a Japanese soldier during World War II who was posted in the Philippines. He was determined never to surrender. Eventually, all of his fellow soldiers were killed except for himself and three others, who all retreated into the wilderness. They lived there for years, conducting raids on police and fishermen when they could. Eventually, they began finding leaflets dropped from airplanes that claimed the war was over, but they thought it was a propaganda trick. They continued their own private war until only Onada was left. He eventually came across a tourist who insisted that the war was over, but Onada didn't know who to trust in a land full of former enemies. He agreed to surrender only if his original commanding officer personally gave him the order. The tourist brought word of Onada's survival back to Japan, the commander was located, and a month later he came to Onada and officially ordered him to surrender. It was March 9th, 1974, and the war had been over for almost 30 years![2] The only person Onada could trust was his commanding officer, whom he finally and gladly obeyed.

For Christians, Jesus is our commanding officer. We may be skeptical of all the other voices in our lives that demand our obedience, but we can trust Him. In our case, the war against sin is over because of what Jesus did on the cross. Obeying Him is an act of surrender in which we lay down our weapons and accept the freedom that comes with His victory.

That kind of obedience doesn't sound so bad, does it?

IN SUMMARY

- Obedience is not a popular idea in our culture because it has been abused.
- The Bible commands us to obey God.
- It's easier to obey someone that loves you and wants what is best for you.
- We can trust God when He asks for our obedience.

PREPARING FOR THE GROUP DISCUSSION

One thing that stood out to me today is:

One question I have based on today's study is:

CLOSING PRAYER

Thank You, God, that I can trust You because of Your love for me. Forgive me for the times I still act in rebellion to You. Please help me to surrender my life to You each day this week as You lead me.

God Will Accomplish His Work Through You

"Truly, truly, I say to you, whoever believes in me will also do the works that I do; and greater works than these will he do, because I am going to the Father."

John 14:12

GOD'S PERFECT RECORD

In 2007, the New England Patriots had a perfect record . . . almost. They won all 16 games on their way to the Superbowl but lost when it mattered most. No matter how hard we try, none of us has a completely perfect record. What about God? Does our imperfection affect the way we see Him?

Have you ever felt like God was asleep on the job? If so, what made you feel this way?

Have you ever looked at your life and the world around you and wondered why God wasn't doing more or doing things differently? Give an example below:

There's a temptation for us to "play God." We think, "If I were God, I wouldn't let _____ happen," or "I don't understand why God doesn't just do _____." Often this frustration crops up during periods when we don't seem to be actively experiencing God's activity in our life.

Experiencing God's activity begins with an understanding of God Himself. He is both all-knowing and all-powerful, which means God knows exactly what must be done to accomplish His purposes, and He has the power to make it happen.

> [9] *"I am God, and there is no other; I am God, and there is none like me.* [10] *I make known the end from the beginning, from ancient times, what is still to come. I say, 'My purpose will stand, and I will do all that I please.'* . . . [11] *What I have said, that I will bring about; what I have planned, that I will do."*

Isaiah 46:9-11, NIV

There is a big difference between knowing that God can do what He wants and expecting that He will do it. The first is head knowledge; the second is genuine faith.

You may want to join God's activity, but are you truly expecting and fully trusting that God can and will accomplish His purposes in your life—no matter how big or scary?

SAFETY NETS

In the hypothetical scenarios below, be honest and choose the response that most closely reflects what you would do.

You are invited to a costume party. Do you:

a) Show up in a crazy costume

b) Text your friends to make sure they're dressing up too

Your student ministry is having a social event. Do you:

a) Plan to attend, no matter what

b) Make sure your best friends are planning on going as well

You feel the Holy Spirit urging you to go forward to pray at the end of a Sunday morning service. Do you:

a) Go to the front immediately

b) Wait for someone else to go first

There is a safety net in standing back and allowing others to take the first step. It's natural to want to know all the variables before we act. But being a disciple of Jesus requires us to follow Him, even if we're the first (or only) one in our friend group to do so.

FANS OR PLAYERS?

Have you ever heard of a bandwagon fan? They always appear whenever a sports team gets off to an unexpectedly fast start to the season. They are along for the ride as long as the team keeps winning. As soon as the winning streak ends, so does the bandwagon fan's support. After all, why invest in something long-term only to be disappointed?

God is not looking for bandwagon fans; He is looking for active and committed players. Unlike a fan, a player doesn't have the option to wait on the sidelines and only jump in when things are already going well. They show up on day one ready to play.

God is at work all around you. If you want to be a part of that work, you need to trust and obey Him. Experiencing God's full purposes in your life comes after obedience. Sometimes we wish walking with God were more like holding a high powered flashlight showing us what is far down the road. Instead, it's more like walking with a lantern, which illuminates just enough for us to take the next step.

"Fans want Jesus to inspire them, but Jesus wants to interfere with their lives."[3]

—Kyle Idleman

In what areas of your faith are you most tempted to "stay on the sidelines?" Why?

In what areas of your life would you rather have a "flashlight" than a "lantern?" Why?

The disciple Thomas doubted the rumor of Jesus's resurrection: "Unless I see in his hands the mark of the nails, and place my finger into the mark of the nails, and place my hand into his side, I will never believe" (John 20:25). A week later Jesus appeared to Thomas, allowing Him to see and touch Him, and Thomas believed. Then Jesus said to him, "Have you believed because you have seen me? Blessed are those who have not seen and yet have believed" (John 20:29).

We don't need to have all the answers or know how our circumstances will turn out in the end; we can trust that God is in control, that He has a perfect plan and the power to accomplish it. When we know the author of the story and trust that He knows best, we don't need to worry about how the story ends. We can follow and allow God to accomplish His mission through us day by day as He reveals His plans one step at a time.

It's okay to have questions like Thomas. What are the biggest questions you have about God, the Bible, or the Christian faith?

THE MOST VIOLENT PRISON IN AMERICA

The Louisiana State Penitentiary (known as "Angola Prison") was not the kind of place you wanted to end up. For years it had been home to thousands of convicted murderers, rapists, and other criminals. Many were on death row, meaning they were just putting in time before being executed for their crimes. Those not scheduled to die could anticipate living out the rest of their lives behind bars. Needless to say, it was a place of hopelessness, which expressed itself in horrific violence and murders within the prison walls.

When a new warden came to Angola, he was shocked by the sense of despair that permeated the place. As a Christian, he knew the only one who could truly bring hope was Jesus. It would require a miracle, but that's exactly what God wanted to do.

After seeking God's direction, the warden introduced the Bible study, *Experiencing God* (the same Bible study that this book is based on), into the prison. God began leading hardened prisoners into a relationship with Himself. Before long, the violence at Angola plummeted a staggering seventy percent. In fact, so many prisoners were feeling God call them to be pastors and missionaries that a Bible college was formed within the prison walls. These new pastors started churches and were transferred as missionaries to other prisons where the violence began to drop as well.

If God can do miracles inside a place as hopeless and violent as Angola Prison, what can He do in and through your life? We all think it would be pretty cool to see miracles, but most of us are not willing to follow God into situations that require miracles. What situations are those? Impossible ones.

Are you ready for God to accomplish the impossible in and through you?

IN SUMMARY

- God has the wisdom and power to accomplish exactly what He wants to do.
- We have the choice of being a fan or a player in God's activity.
- Miracles require impossible situations, and God still does miracles.
- Following Jesus is more like walking with a lantern than with a flashlight.

PREPARING FOR THE GROUP DISCUSSION

One thing that stood out to me today is:

One question I have based on today's study is:

CLOSING PRAYER

Thank You, God, for allowing me to be part of Your amazing activity. Please give me enough light to take the next step forward with You as You accomplish Your purposes through my life.

Never the Same Again

I have been crucified with Christ. It is no longer I who live, but Christ who lives in me. And the life I now live in the flesh I live by faith in the Son of God, who loved me and gave himself for me.

GALATIANS 2:20

DAY 4

CHANGED

In the movie *The Hobbit: An Unexpected Journey*, Gandalf the wizard and Bilbo the hobbit have an important conversation right before they set off on their grand adventure.

Gandalf: "You'll have a tale or two to tell when you come back."

Bilbo: "You can promise that I'll come back?"

Gandalf: "No. And if you do, you will not be the same."[4]

Journeys change people, and we've now reached the end of this eight-week journey. While this book is nearing its end, we pray that this is just the beginning of a lifelong adventure for you.

Experiencing God has been translated into over forty-five different languages. It was recently translated into Mandarin in mainland China. However, there is not an exact equivalent word for "experiencing." The translators asked, "Because this Bible study has changed so many lives here in China, is it okay if we call it 'Never the Same Again.'"

This Bible study is not what changes people; the God it points to is. When you have an experience with God, it changes everything. Take a moment to think back to the start of this Bible study and all you have learned over these last eight weeks.

What is one belief about God that has changed?

What is one belief about yourself that has changed?

What is one belief about your relationship with God that has changed?

A NEW SELF

The Bible is filled with interesting and diverse people. Despite their vast differences, they all have one thing in common: when they came to truly experience God in their life, they were never the same again. It was not just their beliefs that changed; an experience with God radically transformed the way they lived and acted. The apostle Paul described the transformation that occurs this way:

> *22 Put off your old self, which belongs to your former manner of life and is corrupt through deceitful desires, 23 and to be renewed in the spirit of your minds, 24 and to put on the new self, created after the likeness of God in true righteousness and holiness.*
>
> **Ephesians 4:22-24**

Paul was writing from his own experience. He was a terror to the early church, putting many to death. Then he encountered Jesus while traveling to a city called Damascus, and his heart changed along with his behavior. Finally his reputation changed: "They only heard the report: 'The man who formerly persecuted us is now preaching the faith he once tried to destroy.' And they praised God because of me" (Gal. 1:23-24, NIV).

In what areas of your life has Jesus changed the way you live and act?

What areas of your "old self" have you not yet "put off" and surrendered to God?

If you listed anything above, what has kept you from letting go it?

A TRANSFORMATIVE JOURNEY

Over the last eight weeks, we have shared seven important realities with you. These realities are not simply answers for a pop quiz, and they're not just a formula or a theory. They are a map, a path God will lead you down as you come to know and experience His purposes in your life. Each of the Seven Realities are listed in the chart on the following page. Take a walk down the path, and in the right-hand column, write down how the reality relates specifically to you and how you've seen it play out over the last eight weeks.

REALITY 1

God is always at work around you.

REALITY 2

God pursues a continuing love relationship with you that is real and personal.

REALITY 3

God invites you to become involved with Him in His work.

REALITY 4

God speaks by the Holy Spirit through the Bible, prayer, circumstances, and the church to reveal Himself, His purposes, and His ways.

REALITY 5

God's invitation for you to join Him in His work leads to a leap of faith that involves action.

REALITY 6

You must make adjustments in your life to join God in what He is doing.

REALITY 7

You come to know God by experience as you obey Him, and He accomplishes His work through you.

We understand that not all of you are at the same place in your journey. Perhaps some of you have only now realized the amazing truth that God desires a personal relationship with you. Others may have heard God speak and invite you to join His activity but have not yet taken that step of faith to join Him.

Wherever you are along the path, God always has another step for you to take. Are you ready to follow Him wherever He leads? We promise that it will be the best decision you ever make.

IN SUMMARY

- Experiencing God changes everything about us.
- Experiencing God leads us to "put off" our old self and "put on" a new self.
- This book won't change you; but it can point you to God, who will change you.
- God always has another step for you to take on your faith journey.

PREPARING FOR THE GROUP DISCUSSION

One thing that stood out to me today is:

One question I have based on today's study is:

CLOSING PRAYER

Thank You, God, for the journey You have me on right now. Please continue to lead me to experience You and accomplish Your good purposes in my life.

WHILE YOU WATCH

As you watch the video, use the space provided to take notes or write down any thoughts and questions you have.

DISCUSSION

Based on what you learned in the video and in your personal Bible study days throughout the week, spend time discussing the questions below.

What is something that was much different than you thought it would be once you experienced it? How was your experience different from what was in your mind beforehand?

In what ways have your experiences with God impacted your faith?

This week, Mike and Daniel brought up the "Problem of Pain."

Why does the experience of pain make it harder to believe in a loving God?

How have you been able to keep your faith in a loving God despite seeing and experiencing pain in the world?

Obedience was a key topic this week. Mike and Daniel taught that truly experiencing God comes as we obey what God calls us to do.

Why is "obedience" a difficult concept for us to accept?

What gives someone the authority to be obeyed? Why?

In what ways can the concept of obedience be abused?

In what ways is obeying God different from other forms of obedience?

At the end of each day this week you wrote down one main takeaway and one question you had. Take turns sharing one of your takeaways or questions with the group.

SHARE AND REVIEW

The last day of your personal study was titled "Never the Same Again." All throughout the Bible, whenever people had an encounter with God, it left them forever changed. Read how the apostle Paul described this transformation:

> [22] *Put off your old self, which belongs to your former manner of life and is corrupt through deceitful desires,* [23] *and to be renewed in the spirit of your minds,* [24] *and to put on the new self, created after the likeness of God in true righteousness and holiness.*
>
> **Ephesians 4:22-24**

Over the last eight weeks, through our personal study and these group discussions, you have been introduced to seven realities about experiencing all that God desires for your life. As you conclude this Bible study, take some time to review and share what God has been teaching you as you've studied.

What are your biggest takeaways from this Bible study?

Of the seven realities of Experiencing God, which one stands out the most to you? Why?

Which of the realities is the most difficult for you to accept and embrace in your life? Why?

What has God said to you during the last eight weeks?

Based on what you have learned, what is something in your life that you think God is leading you to change?

How has your understanding of God changed?

What questions or doubts do you still have about God or His purposes for your life as you come to the end of this study?

Take the next two minutes to write down what your "next step" is to keep growing in your relationship with God. Make it specific. When you are done, if you feel comfortable, take turns sharing what you wrote with the rest of the group. Commit to encourage and hold each other accountable as you continue to walk this faith journey together.

My next step:

PRAYER & DISMISSAL

As a group, spend some time praying for each other based on the next steps that were shared.

LEADER

GUIDE

TIPS FOR LEADING A SMALL GROUP

1. PRAYERFULLY PREPARE

Prepare for each group session with prayer. Ask the Holy Spirit to work through you and the group discussion as you point to Jesus each week through God's Word.

2. ENCOURAGE DISCUSSION

A good small-group experience has the following characteristics.

EVERYONE PARTICIPATES. Encourage everyone to ask questions, share responses, or read aloud.

NO ONE DOMINATES—NOT EVEN THE LEADER. Be sure your time speaking as a leader takes up less than half your time together as a group. Politely guide discussion if anyone dominates.

DON'T RUSH THROUGH QUESTIONS. Don't feel that a moment of silence is a bad thing. Students often need time to think about their responses to questions they've just heard or to gain courage to share what God is stirring in their hearts.

AFFIRM AND FOLLOW UP ON INPUT. Make sure you point out something true or helpful in a response. Don't just move on. Build community with follow-up questions, asking how other students have experienced similar things or how a truth has shaped their understanding of God and the Bible.

KEEP GOD AND HIS WORD CENTRAL. Opinions and experiences can be helpful, but God has given us the truth. Trust Scripture to be the authority and God's Spirit to work in student's lives. You can't change anyone, but God can. Continually point people to the Word and to active steps of faith.

3. KEEP CONNECTING

Think of ways to connect with students during the week. Participation during the group session always improves when members spend time connecting with one another outside the group sessions. The more people are comfortable with one another the more they'll look forward to being together.

Encourage students with thoughts, commitments, or questions from the session by connecting through texts or social media. Build deeper connection by planning or spontaneously inviting students to get together outside your regularly scheduled group time for a meal, fun activities, fellowships, and projects around your church or community.

4. LEAD GROUP DISCUSSIONS

Thank you for being willing to lead a group of students through *Experiencing God*. If this is your first time leading a group, don't worry. God will work on your heart as you prepare. Here are some helpful tips for preparation:

- Prepare to lead by viewing the videos before meeting with your group and ensure that everything is set up on the day of your meeting. Videos are available at lifeway.com/experiencinggod.

- Review the Group Discussion guide for each week and complete the personal study for the week. (It's really important that you complete the personal study each week. It's important because God will speak to you through it, but it's also important to set an example for the students in your group. If it's not a priority for you, it won't be a priority for them.)

- For the first week, you'll want to familiarize students with the format of the study, including the way the group time will be structured and the features of the *Experiencing God* book (four personal studies each week to be discussed together in your group time after).

- Use the following guides to help you prepare for the Group Discussions.

INTRODUCTION
GROUP DISCUSSION GUIDE

WATCH

Play the "Introduction Video" as you get started. Videos are available at lifeway.com/experiencinggod.

DISCUSSION

In each gathering students will have an opportunity to discuss what they have learned through the video and in their personal study days throughout the week. Spend time discussing the questions from pages 10-11 as students prepare their hearts and minds to begin this Bible study.

GOING DEEPER

Have students grab their Bibles or open a Bible app. Ask volunteers to read the material out loud and discuss the questions together.

As you begin this journey toward experiencing God, let's look at how several characters in the Bible began their own journeys following Jesus. John 1:35-51 tells the story about how Jesus called His first followers.

Discuss questions from page 11-12.

WATCH

Preview Video (Reality 1: God is Always at Work)

PRAYER AND DISMISSAL

Remind students to complete the Personal Study for Reality 1 before next week.

WEEK 2
REALITY 1
GROUP DISCUSSION GUIDE

WATCH

Play the "Reality 1 Video" as you get started. Videos are available at lifeway.com/experiencinggod.

DISCUSSION

Based on what you learned in the video and in your personal Bible study days throughout the week, spend time discussing the questions from pages 32-33.

Mike and Daniel described Christianity as being a character in the exciting story that God—the Divine Director—has been telling since the beginning of time.

At the end of each day this week students wrote down one main takeaway and one question they had. Direct students to take turns sharing one of their takeaways or questions with the others in the group.

GOING DEEPER

Have students grab their Bibles or open a Bible app. Ask volunteers to read the material out loud and discuss the questions together.

For many people today, Christianity is seen as a myth or fantasy. People of faith can even be mocked or made to feel foolish for believing that what the Bible teaches is actually true. Christianity is an exciting story, but it's not just a story. The reason the gospel is called the "good news" is because it's a true story. The apostle Paul even saw clues in nature that pointed to the truth of the Christian story. Read Romans 1:19-20 and discuss the questions from page 33-33.

The disciple Peter understood that some would be skeptical of the story of Jesus. People then, just like people today, did not want to just believe anything. They wanted to have good reasons to believe. Read what Peter wrote in 2 Peter 1:16-21. Discuss the questions from page 35 together.

WATCH

Preview Video (Reality 2: God Pursues)

PRAYER AND DISMISSAL

Remind students to complete the Personal Study for Reality 2 before next week.

REALITY 2
GROUP DISCUSSION GUIDE

WATCH

Play the "Reality 2 Video" as you get started. Videos are available at lifeway.com/experiencinggod.

DISCUSSION

Based on what you learned in the video and in your personal Bible study days throughout the week, spend time discussing the questions from page 54.

This week, Mike and Daniel shared that one of the obstacles that confuses people about the relationship God wants for them is that there are so many different definitions of love presented to us in the world.

At the end of each day this week students wrote down one main takeaway and one question they had. Direct students to take turns sharing one of their takeaways or questions with the others in the group.

GOING DEEPER

Have students grab their Bibles or open a Bible app. Ask volunteers to read the material out loud and discuss the questions together.

Read 1 John 4:16. God is the perfect standard of love. Every other definition of love should be measured against His character to see if it is genuine. This means that if we want to see what love is, we need to look at God. If we want to see how this love is perfectly lived out in a human life, we should look to the example of Jesus. Discuss the questions on page 55.

In 1 Corinthians 13:4-7, which is often read at weddings, Paul was actually referring to how all Christians should treat each other, not just romantic couples. Read 1 Corinthians 13:4-7 and discuss the questions on page 56.

WATCH

Preview Video (Reality 3: God's Invitation)

PRAYER AND DISMISSAL

Remind students to complete the Personal Study for Reality 3 before next week.

REALITY 3
GROUP DISCUSSION GUIDE

WATCH

Play the "Reality 3 Video" as you get started. Videos available at lifeway.com/experiencinggod.

DISCUSSION

Based on what you learned in the video and in your personal Bible study days throughout the week, spend time discussing the questions from pages 76-77.

This week began with a story about Susan being awakened early in the morning with the feeling that God wanted her to call her neighbor. On page 64, students listed three things they would be nervous God might ask them to do. Ask a few students to share some of their answers with the group.

At the end of each day this week students wrote down one main takeaway and one question they had. Direct students to take turns sharing one of their takeaways or questions with the others in the group.

GOING DEEPER

Have students grab their Bibles or open a Bible app. Ask volunteers to read the material out loud and discuss the questions together.

Throughout the Bible, God invited many different kinds of people to join what He was doing: A teenage peasant girl (Mary), a former prince and murderer (Moses), a young shepherd boy (David), a religious zealot (Paul), some blue-collar fisherman (Peter and Andrew), an immigrant (Ruth), a queen (Esther), a government worker (Levi), and the list could go on. In fact, perhaps the only thing they had in common was that they all accepted God's invitation to follow.

When we read the stories about these people in the Bible we might assume that they were very different from us. We see them as Christian superheroes, super spiritual, bold, and with unshakable faith. But the truth is that they struggled with the same fears and insecurities we do. One example of this is with God's invitation to the prophet Jeremiah when he was a young man.

Read Jeremiah 1:4-14 and then discuss the questions on pages 77-79.

WATCH

Preview Video (Reality 4: God Speaks)

PRAYER AND DISMISSAL

Remind students to complete the Personal Study for Reality 4 before next week.

WATCH

Play the "Reality 4 Video" as you get started. Videos are available at lifeway.com/experiencinggod.

DISCUSSION

Based on what you learned in the video and in your personal Bible study days throughout the week, spend time discussing the questions from pages 98-99.

In the video and in your personal study days this week, you learned about four ways that God speaks to people—Bible, prayer, experiences, and the church.

This week began with Mike telling the story of meeting a homeless man named Red.

At the end of each day this week students wrote down one main takeaway and one question they had. Direct students to take turns sharing one of their takeaways or questions with the others in the group.

GOING DEEPER

Have students grab their Bibles or open a Bible app. Ask volunteers to read the material out loud and discuss the questions together.

One of the most important truths in Scripture is not necessarily how God speaks but that He speaks. At the same time, we need to be careful. Claiming "God told me…" can easily be abused to try and justify the things we want to do, rather than the things God is leading us to do. This is why it's important to have the checks-and-balances of these four different ways God speaks—Bible, prayer, experiences, and the church.

As a group, choose one or more of the options on pages 99-101 to study deeper together. If you are a larger group, then you can split up into four smaller groups and each take one, then come back and share your answers together.

WATCH

Preview Video (Reality 5: God's Invitation)

PRAYER AND DISMISSAL

Remind students to complete the Personal Study for Reality 5 before next week.

REALITY 5
GROUP DISCUSSION GUIDE

WATCH

Play the "Reality 5 Video" as you get started. Videos are available at lifeway.com/experiencinggod.

DISCUSSION

Based on what you learned in the video and in your personal Bible study days throughout the week, spend time discussing the questions from pages 120-121.

At the beginning of this week Mike shared how God helped him overcome his fear of becoming a pastor, as well as being diagnosed with type-1 diabetes.

Mike and Daniel used the metaphor of bungee jumping to illustrate the leap of faith. This can be both exciting and terrifying.

Although we like to think of ourselves as rational people, our beliefs are often far more influenced by our emotions and personal experiences (see Jer. 17:9).

At the end of each day this week students wrote down one main takeaway and one question they had. Direct students to take turns sharing one of their takeaways or questions with the others in the group.

GOING DEEPER

Have students grab their Bibles or open a Bible app. Ask volunteers to read the material out loud and discuss the questions together.

Faith is an essential part of being a Christian. Read Hebrews 11:6. Mike and Daniel observed that faith is trusting what you do know in the face of what you don't know. In the Biblical stories, people don't believe truths about God randomly. God reveals Himself to them in some way first.

Hebrews 11:1-40 is sometimes called the "Hall of Faith" because it lists Biblical characters who each walked by faith in amazing ways. Choose one or more of these characters listed on page 122. Read the corresponding verses, and then discuss the questions on page 122. If you are a larger group, you can split up into smaller groups and each take a name from the list to discuss, then come back together to share your thoughts with the rest of the group.

WATCH

Preview Video (Reality 6: Adjustments)

PRAYER AND DISMISSAL

Remind students to complete the Personal Study for Reality 6 before next week.

REALITY 6
GROUP DISCUSSION GUIDE

WATCH

Play the "Reality 6 Video" as you get started. Videos are available at lifeway.com/experiencinggod.

DISCUSSION

Based on what you learned in the video and in your personal Bible study days throughout the week, spend time discussing the questions from pages 142-143.

Mike and Daniel shared this week that you are an "unfinished masterpiece."

Often, when we are misaligned with God, it is because we have chosen to follow after an idol instead of Him. (An idol can be anything that takes the place of God in our lives.)

At the end of each day this week students wrote down one main takeaway and one question they had. Direct students to take turns sharing one of their takeaways or questions with the others in the group.

GOING DEEPER

Have students grab their Bibles or open a Bible app. Ask volunteers to read the material out loud and discuss the questions together.

As you respond to God's invitation to join Him at work in the world, you will need to make adjustments in your life. These adjustments involve both addition and subtraction. There are aspects of your character, thoughts, and actions that God will remove, and also things God wants to add.

No matter how hard we try, the truth is that we'll never be able to make enough changes in our lives to measure up to the goodness God has called us to. The good news is that the Holy Spirit can make those changes in us. Read Galatians 5:16-25 and discuss the questions on page 144.

As the Holy Spirit works to change us from the inside, Jesus also calls us to make some changes in our lives. Read Luke 9:23-24 and answer the questions on page 144.

Together as a group, brainstorm answers to the questions on page 145 for the three areas of adjustments. If you are a larger group, you may also divide into three smaller groups, have each group take one of the areas, and then join back together and share afterwards.

WATCH

Preview Video (Reality 7: Experiencing God)

PRAYER AND DISMISSAL

Remind students to complete the Personal Study for Reality 7 before next week.

REALITY 7
GROUP DISCUSSION GUIDE

WATCH

Play the "Reality 7 Video" as you get started. Videos are available at lifeway.com/experiencinggod.

DISCUSSION

Based on what you learned in the video and in your personal Bible study days throughout the week, spend time discussing the questions from pages 164-165.

This week, Mike and Daniel brought up the "Problem of Pain."

Obedience was a key topic this week. Mike and Daniel taught that truly experiencing God comes as we obey what God calls us to do.

At the end of each day this week students wrote down one main takeaway and one question they had. Direct students to take turns sharing one of their takeaways or questions with the others in the group.

SHARE AND REVIEW

Have students grab their Bibles or open a Bible app. Ask volunteers to read the material out loud and discuss the questions together.

The last day in your workbooks was titled "Never the Same Again." All throughout the Bible, whenever people had an encounter with God, it left them forever changed. Read Ephesians 4:22-24 and discuss the questions from page 166.

Over the last eight weeks, you have been introduced to seven realities about experiencing all that God desires for your life. As you conclude this Bible study, take some time to review and share what God has been teaching you as you've studied.

Take the next two minutes and write down what your next step is to keep growing in your relationship with God. Make it specific. When you are done, if you feel comfortable, take turns sharing what you wrote with the rest of the group. Commit to encourage and hold each other accountable as you continue to walk this faith journey together.

PRAYER AND DISMISSAL

As a group, spend some time praying together for each other based on the next steps that were shared.

7 REALITIES OF EXPERIENCING GOD

1 God is always at work around you.

2 God pursues a continuing love relationship with you that is real and personal.

3 God invites you to become involved with Him in His work.

4 God speaks by the Holy Spirit through the Bible, prayer, circumstances, and the church to reveal Himself, His purposes, and His ways.

5 God's invitation for you to work with Him always leads you to a crisis of belief that requires faith and action.

6 You must make adjustments in your life to join God in what He is doing.

7 You come to know God by experience as you obey Him and He accomplishes His work through you.

MY EXPERIENCING GOD GROUP

You could go through this Bible study book on your own, but we aren't meant to walk with Jesus alone. This is a great opportunity to experience God together with 3-6 friends and form an "Experiencing God" group. As you study God's Word together, challenge each other to live out what you read through discussion, accountability, and prayer. Don't forget to have fun together while doing it.

Who's in your group? Write their names below.

What are 2-3 goals you want to set as a group during your Bible study?

① ② ③

PRAYER REQUESTS

Keep a record of any major prayer requests from your group on this page. Write down the request, the person who asked for prayer, and the date. See what God does in and through your group as you experience God together.

DATE	PERSON & PRAYER REQUEST

SOURCES

Reality 1

1. *The Avengers*, directed by Joss Whedon (2012; Burbank, CA: Walt Disney Studio Motion Pictures, 2012), DVD.

2. Anita Singh, "Daniel Radcliffe: A Cool Nerd," *The Telegraph*, 4 July 2009. Available from the internet: https://www.telegraph.co.uk/culture/harry-potter/5734000/Daniel-Radcliffe-a-cool-nerd.html.

3. Robert Jastrow, *God and the Astronomers* (New York: W. W. Norton, 1992), 107.

4. Blaise Pascal, *Pensees* (New York: Penguin, 1995), 50.

5. Yuval Noah Harari, *Sapiens: A Brief History of Humankind* (New York: HarperCollins, 2015), 24-28.

6. Johnathan Haidt, *The Happiness Hypothesis: Finding Modern Truth in Ancient Wisdom* (New York: Basic Books, 2006), 147.

7. Lin-Manuel Miranda (@Lin_Manuel), "Good morning. You are perfectly cast in your life…," *Twitter*, 29 April 2016. Available from the internet: https://twitter.com/lin_manuel/status/726025564696502272?lang=en.

7. J. R. R. Tolkien, *The Two Towers* (New York: Ballantine Books, 2012), 362.

8. J. R. R. Tolkien, *The Return of the King* (New York: Ballantine Books, 2012).

Reality 2

1. Angela Duckworth, *Grit: The Power of Passion and Perseverance* (New York: Simon & Schuster, 2016).

2. Pascal, 57.

3. Jeremy Nicholas, "Joyce Hatto," *The Guardian* [online], 10 July 2006. Available from the internet: https://www.theguardian.com/news/2006/jul/10/guardianobituaries.artsobituaries1.

4. Robert Putman, *Bowling Alone: The Collapse and Revival of American Community* (New York: Simon & Schuster, 2000), 326.

5. "Zoom Pulls in More Then 200 Million Daily Video Users During Worldwide Lockdown," *Reuters*, 2 April 2020. Available from the internet: https://www.reuters.com/article/us-health-coronavirus-zoom/zoom-pulls-in-more-than-200-million-daily-video-users-during-worldwide-lockdowns-idUSKBN21K1C7.

6. L.W. Hurtado, "God" in *Dictionary of Jesus and the Gospels*, eds. Joel B. Green and Scot McKnight (Downers Grove, IL: InterVarsity Press, 1992), 271.

7. "Cimabue Painting Found in French Kitchen Sets Auction Record," *BBC News*, 27 October 2019. Available from the internet: https://www.bbc.com/news/world-europe-50201691.

8. Zack Pumerantz, "The Fifty Most Inspirational Sports Quotes in History," *Bleacher Report*, 23 April 2021. Available from the internet: https://bleacherreport.com/articles/1156558-the-50-most-inspirational-sports-quotes-in-history.

9. C.S. Lewis, *The Weight of Glory* (New York: HarperOne, 1949), 140.

Reality 3

1. *Aladdin*, directed by Ron Clements and John Musker (1992; Burbank, CA: Buena Vista Pictures, 2002), DVD.

2. Steve R. Parr and Tom Crites, *Why They Stay: Helping Parents and Church Leaders Make Investments That Keep Children and Teens Connected to the Church for a Lifetime* (Bloomington, IN: WestBow Press, 2015), 87-96.

3. Andrew Meola, "Generation Z News: Latest Characteristics, Research, and Facts," *Insider Intelligence*, 29 July 2021. Available from the internet: https://www.businessinsider.com/generation-z.

4. Helen Kooiman Hosier, *100 Christian Women Who Changed The 20th Century* (Grand Rapids: Baker, 2000), 266.

5. C.B. Cebulski (@CBCebulski), "4 dudes giving each other portfolio reviews…," Twitter, 6 July 2016. Available from the internet: https://twitter.com/cbcebulski/status/750887400784748544.

6. Ashley Viens, "Social Media by Generation," *World Economic Forum*, 2 October 2019. Available from the internet: https://www.weforum.org/agenda/2019/10/social-media-use-by-generation/.

Reality 4

1. "Best-selling Book," *Guinness World Records*, accessed 15 December 2021. Available from the internet: https://www.guinnessworldrecords.com/world-records/best-selling-book-of-non-fiction.

2. Daniel Radosh, "The Good Book Business," *The New Yorker*, 10 December 2006. Available from the internet: https://www.newyorker.com/magazine/2006/12/18/the-good-book-business.

3. Craig Blomberg, *Can We Still Believe The Bible? An Evangelical Engagement With Contemporary Questions* (Grand Rapids: BrazosPress, 2014), 17.

4. Lee Strobel, *The Case for Christ: A Journalist's Personal Investigation of the Evidence for Jesus* (Grand Rapids: Zondervan, 1998), 63.

5. Blake Morgan, "Fifty Stats All Marketers Must Know About Gen-Z," *Forbes*, 28 February 2020. Available from the internet: https://www.forbes.com/sites/blakemorgan/2020/02/28/50-stats-all-marketers-must-know-about-gen-z/#67f4053076d0.

6. Matt Novak, "Seven Ghandhi Quotes That Are Totally Fake," *Gizmodo*, 9 July 2015. Available from the internet: https://gizmodo.com/7-gandhi-quotes-that-are-totally-fake-1716503435.

7. "Meet Those Who "Love Jesus but Not the Church," *Barna*, 30 March 2017. Available from the internet: https://www.barna.com/research/meet-love-jesus-not-church/.

8. David Kinnaman, *You Lost Me: Why Young Christians Are Leaving the Church . . . And Rethinking Faith* (Grand Rapids: Baker, 2011), 27.

Reality 5

1. C.S. Lewis, *Mere Christianity* (New York: HarperCollins, 2001), 140.

2. Gary Chapman, *A Teen's Guide to the Five Love Languages: How to Understand Yourself and Improve All Your Relationships* (Chicago: Northfield, 2016).

3. Gary R. Habermas and Michael R. Licona, *The Case for the Resurrection of Jesus* (Grand Rapids: Kregel, 2004).

4. Karen Abbott, "The Daredevil of Niagara Falls," *Smithsonian Magazine*, 18 October 2011. Available from the internet: https://www.smithsonianmag.com/history/the-daredevil-of-niagara-falls-110492884/.

5. Abbott, "The Daredevil of Niagara Fall."

6. Katie Davis, *Kisses From Katie: A Story of Relentless Love and Redemption* (New York: Simon and Schuster, 2011).

7. E. Ray Clendenen, "Fear" in *Holman Illustrated Bible Dictionary* (Nashville: Holman Bible Publishers, 2003), 562.

8. "2010 Chilean Mine Rescue Fast Facts," *CNN*, 1 March 2021. Available from the internet: https://www.cnn.com/2013/07/13/world/americas/chilean-mine-rescue/index.html.

9. David Kinnaman and Gabe Lyons, *Unchristian: What a New Generation Really Thinks About Christianity... And Why It Matters* (Grand Rapids: Baker Books, 2007), 42.

Reality 6

1. "Philip Semour Hoffman Goes Directing," *Interview Magazine*, 14 December 2010. Available from the internet: https://www.interviewmagazine.com/film/philip-seymour-hoffman-jack-goes-boating-marrakech-film-festival.

2. Henry Sheehan, "Cutting Edge," *Directors Guild of America*, Summer 2006. Available from the internet: https://www.dga.org/Craft/DGAQ/All-Articles/0602-Summer-2006/Director-Profile-Alejandro-Gonzalez-Inarritu.aSpx.

3. "Quotes of Michelangelo," *Michelangelo*, [accessed 15 December 15, 2021]. Available from the internet: https://www.michelangelo.org/michelangelo-quotes.jsp.

4. Christian Smith, *Soul Searching: The Religious and Spiritual Lives of American Teenagers* (Oxford: Oxford University Press, 2005), 162.

5. C. S. Lewis, *Mere Christianity* (San Francisco, HarperCollins, 2001), 205.

6. Timothy Keller, *Counterfeit Gods: The Empty Promises of Money, Sex, and Power, and the Only Hope that Matters* (New York: Penguin Books, 2011), xvi.

7. Lecrae, *Unashamed* (Nashville: B & H Books, 2016), 182.

8. C.S. Lewis, *Mere Christianity* (San Francisco: HarperCollins, 2001), 137.

9. Keller, 155.

10. "The Common Sense Census: Media Use by Tweens and Teens," *Common Sense Media*, 3 November 2015. Available from the internet: https://www.commonsensemedia.org/sites/default/files/uploads/research/census_researchreport.pdf.

11. James Clear, "This Coach Improved Every Tiny Thing by 1 Percent and Here's What Happened," *James Clear*, [accessed 15 December 2021]. Available from the internet: https://jamesclear.com/marginal-gains.

12. Marla Tabaka, "Most People Fail to Achieve Their New Year's Resolution," *Inc.*, 7 January 2019. Available from the internet: https://www.inc.com/marla-tabaka/why-set-yourself-up-for-failure-ditch-new-years-resolution-do-this-instead.html.

13. *The Empire Strikes Back*, directed by Irvin Kershner (1980; Los Angeles, CA: 20th Century Fox, 2004), DVD.

Reality 7

1. Jonathan Haidt, *The Happiness Hypothesis: Finding Modern Truth in Ancient Wisdom* (New York: Basic Books, 2006).

2. Rupurt Wingfield-Hayes, "VJ Day: A WWII Hero and a Reckoning with Japan's Past," *BBC News*, 15 August 2020. Available from the internet: https://www.bbc.com/news/world-asia-53763059.

3 Kyle Idleman, *Not a Fan: Becoming a Completely Committed Follower of Jesus* (Grand Rapids: Zondervan, 2011), 31.

4. *The Hobbit: A Unexpected Journey*, directed by Peter Jackson (2012; Burbank, CA: Warner Bros. Pictures, 2012), DVD.

NOTES

NOTES

NOTES

NOTES

NOTES

Get the most from your study.

Is it possible to know God? Can I hear from Him? What does God want me to do? This Bible study has helped millions of believers get answers to those questions.

For thirty years, *Experiencing God* has shown believers how to know God intimately and has encouraged them to step out in faith and join Him in His work—with miraculous results.

This revised version, completely re-written, is set to inspire a new generation of students to know and experience God. This updated study contains the same seven realities of experiencing God as in previous versions, along with new applications, illustrations, and stories from authors Mike and Daniel Blackaby.

This Bible study is designed to help students:

- Recognize God's activity around them.
- Adjust their lives to God and His ways.
- Identify what God wants to do through them.
- Respond to God's activity in their lives.

God has more work to do. Will you join Him?

Want to watch the *Experiencing God* teaching videos when and where it is most convenient? Introducing the Lifeway On Demand app! From your smartphone to your TV, watching videos from Lifeway has never been easier. Visit lifeway.com/experiencinggod or the Lifeway on Demand app to purchase the teaching videos and hear from authors Mike and Daniel Blackaby.

For more information about Lifeway Students, visit lifeway.com/students.

Available in the **Lifeway On Demand** app

Stream on these devices:

ADDITIONAL RESOURCES

EXPERIENCING GOD VIDEO STREAMING BUNDLE
Session videos with authors Mike and Daniel Blackaby teaching the 7 realities of experiencing God.

EXPERIENCING GOD TEEN BIBLE STUDY EBOOK
A digital, 8-session study on knowing and doing the will of God.

EXPERIENCING GOD ADULT BIBLE STUDY BOOK
A 13-session Bible study on the realities of experiencing God. Revised version includes additional material from Richard and Mike Blackaby.